CW01663905

100 PR and Content Ideas for your Business

By Alison Jackson-Carter

First published in Great Britain by Enlighten PR Publishing, 2021

ISBN - 978-1-3999-0826-9

"A good PR story is infinitely more effective than a front page ad."

-Richard Branson

"For most of history, anonymous was a woman."

-Virginia Woolf

"Advertising is saying you're good. PR is getting someone else to say you're good."

-Jean-Louis Gassee

Alison Jackson-Carter is a 'PR Pro' who has spent her career helping people and businesses to share their stories. As a journalist, she spent her 20s working for newspapers, ITV's This Morning *programme, Sky News and 5 News. She then moved into PR where she has worked with hundreds of household brands to increase their media profile.*

Since moving into PR she has led teams who have won awards, launched a successful podcast which has been downloaded more than 100,000 times, and achieved millions of pounds' worth of media coverage for brands.

Her passion for supporting women in business led her to launch Enlighten PR which helps small business owners and entrepreneurs raise their profile and communicate with confidence about their business. In her downtime she can be found listening to The Archers *or trying to read while her children and dog climb all over her.*

Contents

'I don't have anything interesting to say.'

'I think journalists just rely on their friends, don't they?'

'My business is a bit boring.'

'I don't have the time to think of ideas.'

Trust me, I have heard all of this before from small business owners and entrepreneurs. None of it is true.

I have been creating PR stories for brands for more than ten years after leaving journalism. I have worked both at an agency and in-house. In all this time, I have never found a business that my team and I couldn't come up with a PR story for.

But I appreciate that it's really difficult when you are a one-man-band and you are handling your own book-keeping, admin, branding, *Facebook* ads and everything else that comes with running a business. It's easy for me to come up with ideas. I have experience and a great team around me.

So I decided to write this book as a really easy jumping-off point for people to think more creatively about the range of PR opportunities out there for businesses.

Now, not all of these ideas will work for your business. They are also not all ideas that are going to get you on Sky News or the *Good Morning Britain* sofa. But they will all give you a shot at getting national, regional, trade, broadcast or online media. Or they will give you an idea of how you can create some memorable content for your social media channels.

There is no particular order to these and I keep my description and examples brief as most of the ideas are self-explanatory. But I have gone into more detail around some ideas which have the potential to deliver you some serious return on investment.

But before you get started, turn to the back of this book where I have included a PR Strategy Template. I cannot stress enough that your activity needs to have some thought behind it. Don't let the word 'strategy' intimidate you – it's just a plan really. A strategy is just a well thought out plan.

You want to have goals in place and you want to have a clear idea of how those goals will benefit your business. A strategy is where you can also give some thought to the type of media and social media your ideal clients are consuming. If your aim is to use PR to raise awareness of your products and drive sales, and your clients are reading the Daily Mail and never watch TV news, then there isn't much point in you being in the Financial Times or on BBC Newsnight.

If you need help filling in your strategy visit my website www.enlightenpr.co.uk, where you can find a free guide where I break down each section and explain how to fill it in. You can also get a free pitch checklist and watch my webinars explaining how to write a pitch and how to write a press release.

You don't need to hire a PR consultant or an agency. If you want to increase the awareness of your business you can do that yourself. In fact, I would go so far as to say that when you get too big to do it yourself you should hire someone in-house - part-time to start with - over an agency. In my experience, an agency is really useful for supporting a business through a period of crisis or reputation management, or during a period in which the business is looking to build their profile in the investor's market. But that more often than not you are better off with someone in-house.

It will initially feel overwhelming doing the PR yourself, but I promise you that just one hour a week will make a whole lot of difference.

And these ideas will give you some inspiration and save you from having to think of your own ideas!

Love Alison

First things first...What is PR?

There is no shame in not knowing what something is. The shame comes from not acknowledging it and becoming a bullshitter. In my experience, unless you are in the industry, virtually no one knows what it is. So I love it when someone asks me *'what exactly is PR?'*. It's what the girls from The Hills wanted to do, right? What Olivia Pope does? What Patsy and Eddie do?

PR - which stands for public relations - is how you tell the stories of your business to raise awareness of your brand. It is **EARNED** rather than paid for. An advert in a mag-azine or a page of advertorial will cost hundreds of thousands of pounds. An advert on TV could cost you millions. Your *Facebook* ads cost you money. Your membership to net-working groups costs you money. PR does not. It is free.

The PRCA describes PR as how businesses comm-unicate with the public, promote themselves and build a positive reputation and image. How the media represents a brand has a huge influence on how customers perceive it. Customers will always chose a brand they feel they know and trust over an unknown one. So PR is about influencing the media and working collaboratively where possible. By doing this you can help control the narrative around your business. And a proactive PR strategy will help you retain and attract customers.

Most big businesses have in-house PR teams and agency support, all working to tell the right story. But often small- to medium-sized business who can't afford an army of PR strategists don't think about PR. They feel intimidated by it, don't understand it or prefer to stick to marketing which feels more in their control.

PR is not the same as advertising. Essentially the main difference is that you pay for advertising, but you don't pay for PR. PR is earned media coverage, not paid-for media coverage. PR can be part of your marketing mix. Or you could see it as completely separate.

My advice for any small business is that you have to be investing in both. Invest your cash in marketing and your time in PR. Your PR needs will be unique to your business but your PR could include:

· Press coverage

· TV coverage

· Radio coverage

· Social media

· Speaking opportunities - conferences, pod-casts

· Blogs

· Reputation management

Twenty years ago people used to think PR was like *Absolutely Fabulous* while today everyone seems to think it's just about spinning things and telling 'fake' news. While I am sure there are some people who treat PR like that, most publicity and PR practitioners don't engage in lying or covering things up (mostly because you will probably get caught and then your reputation will be impossible to fix).

PR is about **storytelling**, and sometimes your messaging will be around looking at something differently or you will be trying to get attention by doing something unusual, but the reality is that most PR practitioners are just helping brands to have honest conversations with their audiences.

One of the biggest mental roadblocks people have around doing their own PR is the fear that they can't write. **You do not need to be have an MA in creative writing to write.** Anyone can be a writer. You just need to understand what the story is, what the point is, what the **INTERESTING** bit is. With PR you are writing facts, not fiction, and it needs to be simple and honest. You do need a spell checker, though.

PR isn't just a way of brand building and driving sales. It will also build your reputation. If your audience is aware of your brand and work, then one bad review or mistake won't destroy you. Your reputation may take a hit, but your PR will have provided you with a cushion that you can use to bounce back.

PR is cheaper than marketing and will deliver you better, long-term results. And you can do it yourself if you are willing to upskill yourself, jump on to some webinars and learn the basics. If you can master the basics, you can just pay for a PR consultant a few times a year to train you in a new skill, look over your strategy, give you advice on targeting a new audience or help you deal with a reputational issue.

The final thing I want to mention is contacts. You don't need to buy contacts or think that you need to know someone personally before you can email them. Journalists are always looking for stories and contributors. They quite often have their email addresses on the website of the publication they work for. They even have phone numbers! This is because they want people to reach out to them. They want you to contact them if you have something relevant to their audience. By spending just half an hour every week for six weeks, you can create a list of contacts at your target media outlets all by yourself.

Contacts become contacts when you understand what they need and try and give it to them. If you want to build contacts, then don't waste people's time. Do your research and try and help. Journalists are always looking for stories. They aren't going to turn yours down because you haven't schmoozed them over lunch. A black book of contacts helps, but a story is a story. I have friends working at some of the biggest media outlets in the world, but they aren't going to take a story from me if it isn't very good. And I would never ask them to. So don't get put off by thinking you don't have the right contacts. Those email addresses and phone numbers and social media profiles are out there. So go find them!

Proactive or Reactive PR

I like to divide PR into two different approaches: proactive and reactive. Ideally you want to do both. Being proactive is when you proactively try to create news and influence the news agenda. For example, you might issue a press release, create a podcast or share some content. Being reactive is when you react to something in the news agenda, respond to comments and seize opportunities driven by other people.

There is no doubt that I spend the majority of my time being proactive, but the return on investment for reactive PR activity can often appear much higher. An example of this might be spending hours coming up with an idea, writing a press release, getting photos and lining up case studies for a story that then gets a lovely double page spread in a national newspaper - then the next day seeing a story about a celebrity that I can provide expert commentary on. In this situation, I might drop a quick email to the BBC journalist already covering the story, then find that they want me to appear on BBC News Channel. A quick two-minute interview over Zoom then appears on TV every hour for the next six hours. My quote gets used in an article on the BBC website and across local radio.

Because of this some people prefer just to be reactive in their PR approach. If you are always looking for opp-ortunities and keep across the news agenda this can be a great approach. But more often than not you find that you have to be proactive and start getting your name and messaging out there before you get approached for the reactive opportunities.

In this book I have included both proactive and reactive ideas to get you thinking about what's best for you and your business.

A few caveats

- When I talk about the media I am talking about all media outlets: newspapers, TV news, radio, online, podcasts and any other type of media channel that gets invented in the future.
- My general advice is to offer a story to a national news outlet, then to regional, and then create content around it. This is because national news outlets tend to like to get the story first, meaning that they are unlikely to recycle stories that have already been featured in local news.
- PR should be free of charge. If you are paying for media coverage, it's advertising or advertorial.
- You cannot control what a media outlet says about you - but you can influence it. Make sure you are helpful and clear and don't say things you wouldn't like repeated.

- You do not need to write a press release for each of these ideas - you just need a pitch. Do not waste your time writing a press release unless you know how to do it and how to distribute it. You also need to be really confident that you have a story. A pitch is all a journalist needs to tell you whether they are interested and if they want more information. I have a video pinned in my *Facebook* group **Get Seen, Get Heard** which explains why you don't need a press release and how to write a good pitch.
- PR is not sales. If you just want to boast about your sales figures and talk about how brilliant you are, go and phone your nan.
- PR is about getting your message out there and making sure people know you, like you and trust you - because when they do all of this, they will be more likely to buy from you.
- This book is designed to give you ideas and inspiration so that you can start thinking about what PR could do for your business. It is not a substitute for reading the news and building relationships with the press.
- PR is not just media coverage. It is how you interact with your public, your audience, your ideal clients and your key stakeholders.

The Ideas

1. Celebrity stories

The news cycle is dominated by celebrities, and this isn't go-ing to change any time soon. You can see news stories online that feature twenty photos of a celebrity going to get a cup of coffee.

However you feel about the changing face of news, my advice is to lean into it. These stories get printed because they get read. Which means that some of your audience will be reading them.

So - keep an eye on what celebrities are doing and talking about. If an A-lister does something that is in any way relevant to your area of expertise then it is an opportunity to get your brand out there.

When I worked in-house at a consumer law firm we use to use celeb divorce, weddings and custody issues to insert our experts into a developing news story. So when Brad and Angelina broke up we offered broadcast outlets inter-views with divorce lawyers who spoke about what the stages of divorce are and how assets would be divided up.

If a celeb steps out with a noticeably different face or a new hairstyle, that's an opportunity for beauticians, cos-metic surgeons and hairstylists to talk about how they got that look, whether that hairstyle will work on anyone, whether it's a new trend or whether it's something that requires far too much work to catch on. When Bennifer returned, it was an opportunity for brands to talk about other 00s trends that were making a comeback.

If a celeb talks about a new diet, how much they love yoga, or their favourite food - if you are an expert in these things, put yourself out there. Daniel Craig spoke about not leaving any money to his kids before the release of his last Bond film. If you are a financial planner this is where you can offer insight into whether this is increasingly common or is really rare.

Celebs give you lots of opportunities to get your message and expertise out there. Even if it's not something that will get covered by national newspapers or TV outlets, it could be something worth creating a blog or social media post about.

2. Trends

If you are noticing a new trend then insert yourself into the conversation about it. Are behaviours changing? Are young people doing something differently? Are older people doing something that younger people would normally do? Maybe you run a children's business and you have more dads bringing their children than ever before. Why is that? Is it because dads are getting more flexibility from work? Is it because dads are more hands-on? Talk to your customers and find out.

Maybe you service your clients differently from any-one else in the industry because you know they behave diff-erently. Maybe you get most of your business via *TikTok,* for example.

Have you developed something that caters for a post-Covid need? If yellow is the on-trend colour that year and you know that anything you sell in yellow sells out immediately as a result, then talk about it. Maybe you are a fitness instructor and everyone is talking about a certain type of exercise class.

Have your finger on the pulse of what's going on in your industry and talk about it. Major news outlets can often be a bit behind when it comes to trends and what people are doing - so if you are an estate agent and you know that blind offers or gazumping is happening all over the place suddenly then contact your local reporters.

Strictly Come Dancing has created more than ten years of interest in ballroom dancing after decades of it being unfashionable.

Some trends are more obvious than others - like the trend for buying a dog in lockdown. But all trends create talk value and debate. They also all create demand for products.

So look for trends in your industry. Identify them and then talk about them.

HOW TO PITCH IT

The best way to pitch a trend story is to contact the relevant reporter and share with them two things:

1. Data proving the trend
2. Your insight as to why it is suddenly popular

Then offer yourself for interview and, if you can, offer a customer case study. Make sure you and the case study can both be filmed.

3. Newsjacking

Newsjacking is my favourite way of getting media coverage for a brand. You can use it to create content for your social media feeds and your email communications, and it is the easiest and cheapest way to get eyes on your brand.

Sometimes I call it 'commenting' as that's essentially what you are doing. You are commenting on something that is already in the news cycle. You can go as big as you want on something like this. You just have to be agile and content-ready!

The nature of a news story is that it breaks and then it develops and then it gradually disappears. Most only last one news cycle of 12 hours but some last longer and create rich debate and have 'talkability'. The secret to newsjacking is to become part of a breaking story as quicky as possible - a day late and you have missed your opportunity. But if you have something relevant and interesting to say that adds to a breaking news story you can become part of the story.

Newsjacking is a form of real-time branded communication wherein you inject your ideas into a breaking news story at just the right time for it to spread and reach a massive audience.

If you imagine a bell-shaped curve as the lifecycle of a new story then the idea is to inject your content in the news just as the curve is moving upwards. This is the bit before journalists start scrambling for information and people's excitement starts burgeoning. Doing so allows your brand to become a part of the story as it develops into trending news that floods social media platforms and tops *Google* search results.

It's the bit when your expert commentary is a part of the story as much as the images, the case study and the facts.

When I worked for a law firm we used to do this a lot whenever there were celebrity divorces or break ups. We would immediately offer our expertise to 24-hour news channels, national newspapers, newswires, radio stations, anyone who would be covering the story.

By talking about what the stages are of a divorce and what the process was and what the settlements might look like depending on where they filed for divorce, it meant that a celeb break up story could be fleshed out more. By adding the legal insight into the story as soon as it broke, we were able to control some of the story and how it was told.

The key to effective newsjacking is working out what your areas of expertise are. What could you be talking about on the *BBC Breakfast* sofa? Fitness? Fat loss? Yoga? Phonics? Coffee? Teaching? Early years education? Salsa dancing? IT? Earrings? Celebrity news? Sobriety? Once you work out what you are an expert in then you need to start looking for news where your expertise could be part of the story.

Maybe there are statistics out saying that there are fewer women working in IT than any other industry, and you are a woman who works in IT and

you have experience in mentoring and supporting women to pursue IT as a career.
Maybe a celebrity has credited a new diet with a remarkable amount of fat loss and you can talk about the pros and cons of that kind of diet and more effective ways to achieve the same result.

In both of these cases, you can drive people to your website and social media feeds where there is likely to be a huge amount of content that you can be reposting and resharing that can contribute to the story too.

At this point, you might be wondering how you can possibly keep track of all the breaking news stories so that you can be ready to comment on relevant stories.
I have 3 ways to solve this issue for you:

1. Set up real time *Google Alerts* to get notified anytime your area of expertise gets mentioned in the news. Setting them up is easy. I have a blog on my website that will take you through it step by step. They key is to make sure they are niche enough that you don't get inundated. You will also need a *Gmail* account.
2. Read and consume the news first thing in the morning. I know that since the 2020 global pan-demic, a lot of people have found the news to be a cause of great anxiety. A lot of people I have spoken to have switched off and decided they can't face watching and reading the news. But I can't stress how important it is if you want to give yourself the best possible

chance of media coverage. You can't get in the news if you don't understand it.

3. Reach out to planning desks and build contacts. My advice is that you start with five target media outlets and send a VERY short email explaining who you are, what you are an expert in and what kind of topics you can comment on to someone at each outlet. Ask them to keep your details on file as you would love to be considered if they ever need someone with your expertise. Remember that news channels and radio stations have news running 24/7 so they are always in need of guests to talk about current events.

Being the chosen expert to comment in the media is incredibly valuable, and newsjacking is the best way to get the opp-ortunity. The person that contacts the journalist first is likely to be the one that gets the opportunity so it really is fastest finger first.

Another thing I am going to add here is that to be an expert in something you do not need to be the most academically qualified person in the world. You do not need a PhD or 40 years of research experience under your belt. Do not let imposter syndrome stop you looking and seeking out these opportunities. If you do something day-in, day-out, and it is something you are paid to do, then it is no doubt your area of expertise. You experience is what news outlets want to hear about - your insight as someone dealing with these issues every day. Do not let your insecurities hold you back. It won't do you or your business any favours.

4. Datejacking

This is just like newsjacking, but it's when you offer yourself up for comment on awareness days and international days.

Say you are an expert in doughnuts - then you would get yourself out there on National Doughnut Day (the first Friday in June)! If you specialise in women's finances you might offer yourself out on gender pay gap days, or the day in the year when women start working for free because they are paid so much less than men (20th November).

If you are a chef or run children's cookery classes, you might offer yourself up on International Pizza Day (9th February)or National Dessert Day (14th October). It's worth investigating the days relevant to you, which are only a Google search away.

There are days for everything, so I always suggest you just pick a few that are genuinely relevant to your business and brand - ones that your feel passionate about.

Awareness days can offer you opportunities to really have fun with your brand, but they can also be really serious.

If you are selecting a serious one then make sure you give a lot of consideration to the content you are going to produce.

The good thing about annual awareness days is that they come around every year so after a few years you will have content to reuse and repurpose without much effort.

TOP TIP - I downloaded a free calendar of all of the awareness days from **Nina Cresswell**, a copywriter, who is over on *Instagram* @writewell.

5. New starters

It's common for businesses to write a press release when someone new joins their company. In my experience, a new starter pitch will only be relevant to your industry press.

But if you have hired someone with a big network of contacts you definitely want to get the message out there in the industry you work in - whether via the trade press or social media - that they are working with you now.

If you have a new starter with an interesting story, it could also be worth profiling. Maybe they are changing industries, leaving a competitor to join you, or coming to join you because you offer something no one else does. A company I work with is really progressive and has hired a number of staff while they are pregnant. These women then have really powerful stories to tell about how their employer saw their talent and not their personal circumstances. This can create some really positive PR and reinforce the values of your business.

Sharing the stories of your new starters can be a great recruitment tool as well. It's a way of getting people to think about what it would be like to work at your business.

6. New technology

Ok, so I need to caveat this with the fact that it does genuinely have to be new. If you are the first person in your industry to have an app or a client portal, and this tech development makes the lives of your customers a lot easier, then yes, shout about it.

If you are using drones in your photography business as standard or have created an online version of something that has never previously been online, that's interesting. But make sure you know what your competitors are doing.

So many businesses live in a bubble where they think what they are doing is amazing while not realising that it's industry standard. Also, think about whether the tech actually helps your customers or not. If it doesn't then maybe it's an internal story more than an external one.

It's easy to get wowed by your own technology - as it will often make your life much easier - but it needs to really change the way that customers work with your business. It needs to make their life easier and better.

7. New branding

This might not be one for mass media unless you are a HUGE outfit with a much-loved and well-known brand. But there is still a lot of content that can be created around your new branding.

Bring your audience on the journey with you - tell them why you want a new brand, what you want it to say about you, and ask for feedback. There is always the poss-ibility that the new brand might have an amazing story behind it; in which case tell it! Your branding says a lot about who you are as a business.

It can be cheeky and show your sense of humour. It can show your values and raise awareness of your business.

New branding can also be an opportunity to refresh your purpose, mission, values and your general business messaging.

For help with branding I recommend your join **Sarah Monte-Colombo's** *Facebook* group *Brandsetters and Goalgetters.*

For help with your messaging I recommend you follow *J. Nichole Smith: Building Brands that Matter* on *Facebook.*

8. New agencies

This can be an easy way to get your business out there: hiring an agency to work for you, whether that's a digital agency, a PR agency or an advertising agency. Agencies love to promote their client roster, so let them.

Even freelancers and consultants love to shout about who they are working with on social media. Let them tell everyone and broadcast the fact they are working with you.

You can collaborate and support each other with social media posts and recommendations that help both of you to get the message out there. You reach their audience and they reach yours. Win-win.

Don't feel obliged to hire an agency, though. Put your business first, especially if you have brought someone on board to support you with a problem. If someone hired me to help with crisis communications or reputation management, I would expect them to want discretion and ask me to sign a nondisclosure agreement. If you want to work with someone closely and they will be given information about your business that others would like to have, then don't feel that you can't ask for confidentiality.

9. Promotions

Depending on the industry you work in, you will find that internal promotions are news for the trade press. Senior roles in big businesses are interesting for industry media.

It's even better if there is a great story behind that promotion. Maybe someone is returning to the work force after a sabbatical or studying; maybe they come from an interesting background or are returning to work after a period out to raise their children.

It's always fascinating to hear from people who have got to a senor role via an unusual route like an apprenticeship.

If you have a trade magazine that is interested in content like this, then my suggestion is to wrap a few promotions into the same pitch or press release. That way you are also highlighting that you have good, clear, achievable career paths in your business.

10. CSR activity

CSR stands for Corporate Social Responsibility, so is shorthand for charity fundraising or community service work. So many businesses do some fantastic CSR activity but fail to ensure it aligns with their business values or resonates with their ideal client.

If your business is a food business, then donate your unsold food to homeless shelters - don't do a fun run for a cancer charity. If you are a law firm, donate some of your time to helping people that's cannot afford legal representation. If you are a phonics class, then do something to encourage childhood literacy. If you run a wellness business, donate some of your time and facilities to women that have been through something traumatic or life changing. Do something that ties in with your area of expertise if you can.

When you are thinking about getting any PR benefit from CSR activity focus it on the people who will benefit from what you are doing. No one wants to see three middle aged people in business dress holding a novelty cheque. They want to see children using the playground equipment the money from that cheque paid for.

You can remind your audience of your purpose and values, of course, but keep the focus on the people benefiting - not your business.

11. Employee achievements

Have any of your employees done something amazing? Perhaps they got top marks in an industry exam. Perhaps they have broken a world record or written a book or been featured on TV. Maybe they are such an expert in something they have been advising scriptwriters of *The Archers* or *EastEnders* on a big plotline.

Talk to your team regularly and find out what they are doing outside of work. You could have people with fascinating interested and achievements outside of their day job that you can celebrate through your PR and content.

Your employees are brand ambassadors for your business and you should help raise the visibility of their achievements.

12. Employee charity work

People are always coming up with creative ways to raise money for charities that are important to them.

A colleague I once worked with ran 12 marathons - 12!!! - to raise money for a charity that supported victims of child sexual abuse. She worked as a solicitor helping survivors of child abuse, so she was passionate about doing what she could to help. This is an example of how people can be so moved by the work they do that they decide to raise money for good causes.

We helped this employee get media coverage where she shared her story and that drove donations to her *Just Giving* page. It also mentioned the firm and the work she did and how the business had encouraged and supported her.

So make sure you know what kind of charity work your colleagues are involved in and make sure you share it with your audience.

13. Sponsorship

If your ideal client is in your local area, then you may think about sponsoring a local sports team. If they are also parents, consider sponsoring the kids' football club or gymnastics club.

There are sports organisations that are crying out for funding and this can easily be a win/win situation.

If you are a bar that relies on students drinking and eating at your establishment, then consider sponsoring one of their popular teams - rugby, cheerleading, hockey.

It's an easy way to get eyes on your brand while helping out a local group.

14. Brand collaborations

These can work really well when you have different audiences as it can open you up to a whole new audience. Alternatively, it can be a great way of showing your customer how much you understand them

Lego show their audience they understand them all the time by teaming up with what other big brands doing for maximum impact: *Star Wars, Harry Potter, Ghostbusters, The Simpsons, Batman* - they have done a lot of brand co-llaborations and they reinforce their brand with their ideal clients.

Marks and Spencer working with Holly Willoughby was a great collaboration too. Most of Holly's fanbase wouldn't have thought of shopping at *M&S* until she launched her first collection of 'must haves' with them. So *M&S* have a whole new generations of customers coming in the door.

If you make notepads, find someone like a poet to add some poetry into your designs as a limited edition - or a handbag designer who can work with you so your notebooks match their bags. If you make or sell chocolates, collaborate with a wine seller who can pair the perfect wine with your chocolates. If you run a children's music class, then collaborate with a children's class that's focused on sport.

Big brands do this all the time. It's a great way to tap into their following and build the awareness of your brand.

15 -17 Research

I absolutely love using research for PR. Research stories are really common in the news - you probably read them all the time. They usually lead with a headline like '8 out of ten students can't cook a tin of beans' or 'Brits now prefer going to the gym to going to the pub'. It might not be clear at first, but these are always PR stories being driven by a brand. Here is how it works:

1. A brand or company uses a research method, usually a survey, to produce some data (more on different ways to do this below). This data says something interesting about people's habits or tastes and is often divided by pitting men against women, or the older generation against youngsters. For example, perhaps you carry out some research and discover that more people than ever are suddenly doing a lot of home-growing their own veg in their gardens.
2. Newspapers and websites are keen to write about the story that the data tells, because it's usually either a) amusing, b) surprising or c) both (these kinds of stories are often light-hearted, but research can also be used to demonstrate important and shocking realities about our society - more on this below).
3. Journalists and news sites are really happy to use the data you have collected as content,

because it's very little effort – after all, you've done all the work, so that's an easy page of news for them. As a fair trade-off for using your research, the journalist or news site will print your brand name, usually in a phrase like 'A recent survey carried out by Sunflower Garden Design shows that…'

4. In place of, or in addition to this, you can now be inserted into the article as an expert voice on your own data: 'Susan Smith, the owner of Sunflower Garden Design, said, 'It's no surprise that more people are growing their own veg in these times,' etc.

Brands either do research really well or they really struggle. The mistake they often make is that they focus on the statistics and not the story. The stats need to be the proof points of an interesting story or trend that feels relevant and truthful. Stats themselves won't make a good news story. The key is the story the stats tell.

The PR value to you is the name-check itself – the publishing of your name or your brand's name and the key messages you want to communicate to your audience in the quotes. Once again, it is NOT advertising, so Susan from Sunflower Garden Design does NOT need to start plugging her services at this point – and at any rate, the journalist won't print it.

There are three types of research you can use for PR purposes:

1. You can commission research through an MRS-accredited research company.
2. You can piggyback off of someone else's research.
3. you can look at your own data.

So let's go through the pros and cons of each.

Commissioning your own research

Research works when you want to help bring an issue to people's attention or highlight something relevant to your business or audience.

When I first started working with a law firm, I spoke to their employment lawyers, and they told me that they were called by women who had been victims of maternity discrimination - women who were fired from their jobs for getting pregnant or taking maternity leave; mums who were sidelined when they tried to return to their roles. I immediately wanted to talk to these women and highlight the issue, but women who allege maternity discrimination more often than not end up being offered a settlement of cash to leave the business and, in return, sign a confidentiality agreement - so none of them could share or talk about their experiences. Not with anyone. Just their immediate family and GP. So not their friends, their wider family or anyone else that might be struggling with the same issues, even with the same employer.

So how could I highlight the issue when no one could talk about it?

I commissioned some research. The statistics we got back about the amount of women forced out of their jobs was shocking, and we led the media narrative on this issue for years after (if you want to learn more about maternity discrimination please follow *@pregnant_then_screwed* on *Instagram* and the amazing work of **Joeli Brearley**).

If you want to give yourself the best chance of getting blanket coverage, you will need to commission your own research through a proper research agency. I only ever use *Censuswide*. I have known the MD **Nicky Marks** for the best part of fifteen years, and I trust her to not only give me the best price but also the best customer service. *Censuswide* are MRS-accredited which means that all of the major news outlets are happy to take their research (MRS stands for the Market Research Society). Their surveys are nationally representative and go through rigorous testing to make sure that the results are thorough and stand up to scrutiny.

Nicky and her team understand why people use research for PR purposes and they will tell you if they think you won't get the results you think you will.

If you want to commission research to get stats that say that people prefer playing board games to watching TV, then they will tell you that they think you are unlikely to get that stat back. The last thing you want to do is commission research to prove a point and show that something is a trend only to find out that the stats come back and you are wrong.

So it's crucial to have an agency that will be honest with you. Nicky and her team are running hundreds of thousands of research project a year so they understand people better than anyone, and they have a good instinct for how their panel of respondents will answer questions. Generally you want 2,000 respondents for a survey to be taken seriously. You also need at least 10 questions but if you want to do it properly I would advise about 15-20.

My advice is to also consider what you want your press release to look like in advance and share that with the agency. Tell them WHAT you are trying to uncover. Is it that more people have a side hustle than ever before? Is it that dads feel uncomfortable attending baby classes? Is it that no one eats a full English breakfast any more? They can help you establish whether your idea is viable from a data perspective. Then you can focus on making sure you have all the stats to tell a story. You need to have the reasons WHY something is happening, WHO it is happening to and WHERE it is happening.

My advice is to explore question formats. If offering multiple options, make sure that people can tick several boxes in one go rather than being limited to just one. This provides more information and therefore more data to play with.

Also, try ranking questions. If you ask people to name their favourite condiment, you'll get a thousand replies of tomato ketchup. But if you give five options and ask people to rank their favourites, and mustard comes fifth, well, you have two ways of looking at that data: either mustard is everyone's *least* favourite condiment, OR mustard is the fifth *most popular* condiment (not bad). Ranking questions give you more wiggle room for your numbers.

Averages are brilliant for giving you a conversation starter around whether people do something more or less than the average person,

This kind of research is going to set you back around £3k. That's not small change for a small business, I know. Which brings me to my second research idea.

Use Someone Else's Research

The Office of National Statistics (ONS) is constantly releasing new data. They also let you know what they are releasing in advance of releasing it - so you can sign up for relevant alerts on their website.

Alternatively you can do a *Google* search to see if they have released stats related to your area of expertise in the past and then wait for them to do it again. Sometime your competitors will release data that you can comment on and really annoy them.

Or an industry body may release data or insights. Keep across what your industry are doing and if there is any data you can use in your PR and content.

Use Your Own Data

And finally, you can look at your own data. If you have a large and engaged email list, *Facebook* group or *Instagram* following you could look to survey your own audience. The stats may not stand up to press scrutiny, but if you can say you polled 20,000 mums and they all thought 'x' or hated 'y', then a large sample size like that could get you coverage.

Even if they don't give you press coverage, they could give you a lot of ideas for content as well as insights into your audience and what makes them tick.

18. Mergers and acquisitions

If you are merging with another business, or acquiring one, this is a perfect opportunity to build your audience and your pool of brand ambassadors. I would always advise that people consult with professional PR consultants when it comes to M&A as it can be a stressful period. Thinking about internal and external communications might not be the top of your to-do list, but it needs to be - it's often as important as the legalities if there are a lot of employees involved.

My one piece of advice to anyone managing it themselves is to win the hearts and minds of the people who are coming into your business before thinking about your external PR. Internal communication should come first here. Having your business acquired is an extremely unsettling period and not one that you should underestimate.

You can celebrate your growth and scale in the media at a later date. Try and control the narrative and hold off from making it a positive story unless it truly is a positive story for all of the stakeholders involved. When you feel ready to announce and start talking externally, make sure you talk about how the merger will impact customers and make a difference to them.

19. New offices

New offices or premises make for good news stories as local papers LOVE celebrating any business that is opening in the local town or city. If it's a high street location, even better.

It shows you are investing in the area, you are bringing people and therefore trade into the city and it's something that local media will likely be happy to cover.

In your pitch you can use the new shop space as an opportunity to talk about the growth of your business and how you service your customers and how they will have a better experience once your new premises open.

Stories like this can also make you look like an attractive employer with a nice place to work, therefore helping with your recruitment efforts.

20. Unusual requests

I use this example a lot in training sessions so anyone who has attended one will be familiar with it. *Travelodge* do a regular round-up of the most unusual requests they get at their hotels. It always creates a lot of media coverage as it's one of the 'Brits are thick' stories that people love to read.

Here are some of the requests they have had.

Is Haggis an animal?
What time do the Northern Lights come on?
Can you ask the seagulls to be quiet?
What train do I get from Kings Cross to get to Hogwarts?
Can you arrange for the moon to look into my room as I want to propose to my girlfriend under the moonlight?

If you work in a business where you get a lot of unusual requests from the public then it might be worth keeping track of them and creating some PR about it.

You can use a story like this to get across the fact that while you love going above and beyond for your customers there are some things you can't help with. It makes you look like you listen to your customers but also are able to have a sense of humour about things.

21. Recruitment drives

Local and regional media love to hear that businesses are investing in their community - so if you are launching a new business, office, or restaurant, and you need 10 or more staff to launch it, then it might be worth talking to the local media.

They will often cover every stage of your launch that way, from seeking planning permission, to fitting out the premises, to hiring and launching. It's a great way to engage with the local community and show them what you are all about, especially if you are bringing something new to the area.

Perhaps you are struggling to find new recruits for your business or you have a unique interview or application process. There could be an opportunity to tell an interesting story.

22. Interesting job roles

The media love to hear from people that get paid to do something unusual. *Pizza Express* were all over the news when they hired a 'tommelier' - someone whose full-time job was to taste tomatoes and recommend the best ones for each pizza.

The story presented *Pizza Express* as a restaurant that prioritised and invested in sourcing the best possible ingredients for their food. It highlighted their passion for high quality food and also made people think 'wow, I could do that job!'

Silentnight got good coverage when they announced they were looking to hire pillow and mattress testers that they would pay £300 a night. They also gave their testers a free Netflix subscription and let them keep the products. They said that, as their mission was to help people sleep better, they were after applicants who would take the role seriously. You could apply via their website.

This kind of story is a great way to get the media to tell people about how important quality and good results are for your business.

Lots of businesses do this on a smaller scale on social media by hiring 'brand ambassadors' - people who get products for free or at a discount if they share images, stories and video of them being used. Think about whether you need any new staff to help with quality control in your business - even if it's just a short-term role.

23. Financial success

Often your industry press will be interested in your financial performance. This is an opportunity to make your business look attractive to investors and also highlight your leadership skills.

If you have had a strong year and your business is going from strength to strength, you may want to use your performance to instil confidence in all of your stakeholders. My advice is to always position your financial success in terms of your customers, your staff and your continued investment into the business. Also be mindful that if you are celebrating your financial success you should be aware of what and groups of dissatisfied staff or customers will think.

Within financial results it's worth adding in some words about your corporate and social responsibility work.

24. Investment

If you are attracting investment, then this may be something you want to promote. If your investors are happy to have publicity, it's a great way to make more people consider investing in you.

This is the same for grants. I remember covering the grants that people were given by the Prince's Trust when I was a junior reporter in the local press.

If someone thinks your business is worth investing or giving money to, then it is definitely something to celebrate.

25. Sales milestones

Have you just cut your 1,000th customer's hair? Have you just sold your 10,000th pair of earrings? Is this your 50th franchise opening? All of these milestones could make a nice story about your business for regional media outlets. They can also make brilliant pieces of content, especially if you offer all of your customers a discount on the day of your milestone or run a giveaway to celebrate your success with them.

If you have a product which is particularly unique or expensive or part of a 'trend' or has sold out in a matter of hours, that could be interesting too. Perhaps a Japanese influencer bought your product and you sold out of all your stock overnight - that would be a fun story.

26. Customer stories

This is when your customer is the story. This is one of the best possible ways to get PR for your business. Who is better to talk about how great your business in than a happy customer?

Businesses often have customers who achieve great things. A PT might have a client who has had an incredible weight loss transformation story. A school might have a story about a pupil who won a prestigious chess tournament. A pregnancy class might have a story about a woman giving birth in a class. A shop might have a story about a customer who saved the life of somebody who collapsed in the store. These stories can be a great way for you to be celebrating the people who use your business while also getting your name and messaging out there too.

Clients are the best way to show how you can help people! If you help them get their story out there the journalist will normally be more than happy to include a comment from you. And your customer stories and success provide great content for your social media channels and your testimonials page on your website.

On social media I follow a children's theatre company and they are really good at celebrating the successes of their pupils outside of the theatre school, whether that's charity fundraising, school achievements, modelling jobs, passing exams, leaving school etc.

She recently posted about a pupil that donated her hair to a charity. The children are tagged in the posts, their parents share the posts and engage with them and it shows she really cares about her students.

Maybe one of your regular clients has a powerful story to tell or has done something amazing. You can help them share their story and become part of it. So look at your customers and ask questions. Maybe you notice that a man has bought earrings from you every month for 18 months and you reach out to him and it turns out he is in a long distanced relationship because he is isolating with a vulnerable relative or is stuck in another country and is sending them to his girlfriend every month as a gift. He buys her earrings as they are one thing he can see when they *Zoom* or *Facetime*. That's a lovely story he might let you share.

Maybe you have three generations of one family where all the women buy and wear your earrings. That would make a lovely photo opportunity. Be nosy. Ask questions. Talk to your customers. If they tag you on social look at their profiles. Follow them the same way they follow you.

One question I always get asked here is how people can approach their customers to share their story with the press. Don't overthink this. I am constantly surprised by the amount of people willing to talk to journalists and share private details from their life! In one of my jobs a man lost his manhood in a horrific accident and was quite keen to share his story with the press! People - especially women and mums – like to share information about terrible things that happen to them to warn other women not to make the same mistake. They also love sharing success stories and life hacks to make each other's lives easier. If you are a member of any mums' *Facebook* groups, you will know this.

When my two-year-old broke his arm on a trampoline I was mortified - but I also told everyone. I genuinely thought that children only broke limbs on trampolines by falling off, so the idea that you could just bounce and land wrong while still on the trampoline and still break your arm badly shocked and scared me. So I told everyone I could so that they wouldn't make the same mistake. And anyone who has an *NCT* or school *Whatsapp* group knows that people share information with each other constantly to help each other.

So don't be afraid to ask someone to share their story. They will be more likely to say yes than you think!

27. Freebies to journos

There is no doubt that freebies can garner you news coverage. It makes sense. For someone to write about your product they need to know how it works, whether it does what you say it does and basically whether it's any good.

But this area is fraught with difficulties, because media outlets are inundated with freebies.

When I was at *This Morning* there were rooms the size of an average flat full of things that were sent in by PR people. Every six months they would run a charity sale for staff, where people could buy these freebies, with the money being donated to a good cause.

Even when I was working on a local newspaper we would get free meals at local restaurants in exchange for a review. So if you are sending out freebies you COULD secure some great coverage. But you could also end up significantly out of pocket.

This is why the rise of influencers has been so huge. Because paying for a sponsored post with a relevant influencers can be more cost effective. So if you host a class or run an event and there isn't a great loss to your business then it could be worth offering freebies. But if you products are costly then I would be a lot more cautious.

As a side note if you are ever approached by someone and asked to provide a freebie then get it in writing that your business will be credited. Because there isn't much point to your product being featured otherwise.

TOP TIP - Don't just think about targeting journos for freebies. Give them to your ideal clients. **Charlie Day** owns *Phonics with Robot Reg* and she had two children's entertainers at her son's birthday party. One was a franchisee for this business. I didn't know Charlie well at the time but my son and her son were friends from preschool. I had always thought phonics classes sounded boring but they were AMAZING. Off the back of that birthday party I signed up for 18 months of phonics classes with my youngest son. My cousin then took her twins. And I rave about those classes to anyone who will listen. We did the online classes during lockdown, we have our very own Robot Reg teddy at home as well as all the props for the classes too.

Not only was I Charlie's ideal client, but she knew she had an amazing product and that word of mouth would be fantastic for her business. My youngest isn't yet four and he loves phonics now, as well as being streets ahead of others when it comes to reading and spelling.

28. Industry awards

These are a great way to raise your profile in your industry. But they have very little currency outside of your industry.

So yes, if your target audience is in your industry then you should invest the time and money into this. But if not I would give it a miss.

I have won PRCA, CIPR and Corporate Content Awards - hell yes, I told you I was PR Pro - but those awards will be meaningless to anyone who isn't in the PR industry. If you win an award you should definitely try and get some coverage in your industry press but beyond this it may well be one for your social pages and website.

29. Industry rankings

Not every industry has these, but some have rankings where a trade publication will rank the top 100 businesses or products. This could be something you are asked to submit an entry for, or one that they will compile without your input.

The legal industry is full of them. *The Lawyer* Hot 100 lawyers, The Top 100 UK firms, The Top 250 International Firms - it can be a full time job keeping track of them all. I would always look for the kind of rankings that exist in your industry and look for ways in which you could be get involved. Engage with the people compiling the lists and talk about how you can get on them.

If the customer experience is an integral part of your business USP and values, then look for industry rankings around the best providers of customer service.

30. Quick wins in communities

Quick wins are when you see something has happened in your local area that is getting some attention and you try and help. Maybe a block of flats suffers a fire and there are homeless people who are being moved to emergency accommodation. If you are a restaurant you might send them fresh food parcels. If you sell clothes you might donate a clothing parcel to help them.

It could be anything to support families in your local communities, especially if families are your target audience. You could fundraise for them or donate a day's profits. If you are a window repair business and the local charity shop has their window smashed, you could replace it free of charge. If a local school has a break-in and something is stolen that you could help replace, get involved.

If there is a cause you can get behind in your community, do it - especially if it's a way to talk about what you offer and do. Try and build links with churches, schools and community facilities and see where you can give back.

If it's a significant event you may find that the local newspapers, TV and radio stations are covering it and happy to include you as part of the story.

31. Anniversaries

These are opportunities for you to celebrate your business and your values, and an excuse to remind people what you are all about. Treat your business birthday like you would your child's birthday party. Get balloons, tell everyone on your social media channels, have a party, email your database and offer a discount. Thank your staff, thank your customers, thank your family for supporting your dream.
And through all of this content your company values will shine through in a really infectious way.

You can mark the anniversary of your business, or maybe even your signature or bestselling product - or the date you moved in to your shop space. Your local paper may be interested in supporting your anniversary, especially if it is a significant one.

32. Client story follow-ups

If you ever share interesting and topical customer stories makes sure that you look for ways in which you can do a follow-up. A follow-up is when you revisit something that you have covered before. Think about whether there is an update on the story or whether there is more to tell.

If you have shared a client success story then make sure that you share their future success.

For example, if you share a weight loss story then if that person goes on to run a marathon or do a triathlon or enter a bikini body building competition, then make sure you keep telling that story.

33. Founder stories

I was reluctant to put this one in here as so many times I talk to entrepreneurs who seem to think that the only story they can tell about their business is the one about why they set it up. I don't know where this idea came from, and as you can see from this book, there are hundreds of different stories people can tell about their businesses.

But the founder story is certainly one of them. The key to it being a really great story is for it to involve a relatable journey. I was listening to one of my local business owners tell their story once, and I was pretty gripped. It went something like this –

"I decided on a bit of a whim that I wanted a shop but the rent was pretty high. I was thinking about it but wasn't too sure as it seemed like a big risk but then my dad said to me one night – 'guess what, I bought that shop for you' and I was sooo happy. It basically worked out really well for him from a tax perspective...."

That's great if your dad has a lot of spare cash to invest in your business idea. But not many people can relate to that.

A better story would have been...

'My dad came in and said to me one night 'I just heard that shop has gone to someone else'. I was totally gutted. It wasn't until the shop was gone that I realised how much I really wanted it but that I was letting my fear hold me back.

So after that I spoke to all the estate agents in that area and told them to call me when the next property came up and I set to work on a business plan so as soon as one was available I could get to work'.

See what I did there? One was relatable, included a moment of truth and demonstrated that succeeding in business is hard work and had ups and downs. Alan Sugar is always telling everyone how he started out on a market stall. Everyone knows the stories about Bill Gates and Steve Jobs working away in their garages. Think about it for a moment - how come we all know those stories? It's because their brands got those narratives out there, into the public, so we would be reminded that there were hardworking, struggling people, just like you and me, behind the yachts and private islands. Lisa Johnson and Leona Burton have great stories about their backgrounds and how they overcame a lot of hurdles to get where they are now. If you have a great story that will inspire people, then share it. But please put your journey into perspective.

34. Thought leadership

Anyone running a business is an expert in their field. By sharing that expertise and providing solutions to problems and context to topical issues, you can become a thought leader. Thought leadership is what a lot of bloggers do. It's providing the depth of your knowledge of something into digestible pieces of content that answers questions that people have.

It's an opportunity to educate, inform and inspire.

If people ask you the same questions over and over, then create content with the answer. If it's something that's topical, you can offer that content to a media outlet. It doesn't need to be written content. It could be video, a podcast or an infographic. Think about how many different ways you can use the same messaging across all of those different formats.

The important thing is to get your thoughts out there to establish yourself as an authority.

35. Responding to customer feedback

This is a great way to show that you are listening to your customers and what a great company you are. If you get feedback from a customer who loved the necklace they bought from you, but that their 5 year old daughter loves it too and keeps stealing it, then make a big deal of it. Reach out to them and make a child's size necklace so they can match. In fact, go further and share the story on social, and see if your customers think you should have a mini-me range.

If a child leaves you a review and says you need to have more ice cream flavours on offer, then make sure that next time they come in you blow their mind with the selection. In 2019 a young girl wrote to *Tesco* complaining that the school uniform options for girls had fake pockets on their trousers while the boys ones had real pockets. *Tesco* saw this as an opportunity rather than a criticism and responded very quickly with a letter from a Customer Services Specialist who said he could understand her frustration. He said he was forwarding the letter to the Clothing Buyers team and gave her a £10 gift voucher.

The story was featured everywhere and opened up a great discussion on how girls' and boys' clothing differs like this in most stores.

36. Open days/Launch parties

Events can be a great way to get attention. If you are offering free drinks, food or stuff people will bite off your hand to attend. Post-lockdown, people are desperate for face-to-face interaction, and to do things with other people, so now is the perfect time to plan something. A launch party for your key stakeholders (customers/suppliers/industry figures/journalists/investors) can be a great way of raising awareness of what you do and an opportunity to promote a new product.

An open day can be an opportunity for people to meet you and your colleagues and really get a feel for your business. PR isn't always about media coverage but about raising awareness of your business. Parties and events are perfect for this.

37. Controversy

There is no doubt that creating a bit of controversy can secure you headlines and get people talking about your business. Some brands like *Paddy Power* embrace it, while most shy away from this kind of activity in case it offends their audiences.

I think that if you have a global brand with a clear purpose then it's fine to be a bit provocative every now and again. But you need to be prepared for any backlash and have your responses drafted in advance, Make sure anything you do or so has buy in from all of your senior stakeholders and test it with focus groups first.

Gillette created a controversial ad in 2019 that played on its tagline *'The Best a Man Can Get'* by showing images of sexual harassment, sexism in the workplace and violence between teenage boys. It then shows people stopping these behaviours. It's great to see a high-profile business using it's platform and budget to raise awareness of social issues. But not everyone likes the advert. There was criticism at the time that it emasculated men. But a business like *Gillette* would have thought that alienating some of their audience was a calculated risk for the benefit of giving their brand a clear identity. It also is likely to be received well by the harder-to-reach under 25-audiences who - research shows - like brand that have a clear purpose.

Some brands like to create controversy by 'testing' something or 'considering' something. *M&S* announced they were considering charging more for bigger bras. This created a lot of headlines and outrage so they quickly reversed their decision. But this news had coincided with *M&S* rebooting its bra selection with more modern designs. The story also highlighted that they service women with bigger breasts - not all shops do. It created great media coverage as well as giving newspapers and media outlets a reason to legitimately publish photos of women with big boobs wearing bras. A PR campaign like this would have cost significantly less than buying advertising space.

Ryanair famously announced they were going to charge passengers if they wated to use their toilets in 2010. Headlines were everywhere declaring *'You have to spend a pound to spend a penny'*. This created headlines all over and didn't cost the business anything. They also extended the life of the story by then changing their minds, just like *M&S* did. *Ryanair* - as a budget airline - have always had a small marketing budget so are creative with their use of PR over advertising spend.

Controversy works because it creates talk-ability. The best kind of PR activity is one that gets people talking and the best way to do this is to create an emotional response in people about whether some-thing is fair or unfair. It creates debate.

If you are thinking about creating some controversy think about something that might be seen as taboo or shocking but is also something people will agree with. And remember you don't have to implement it. You could just say you are considering doing something and see what kind of reaction you get.

38. Social movements

If your brand has a reason to attach itself to a social movement, this can be a great way of getting eyes on your brand while explaining your purpose and mission.

Climate change and sustainability are great examples of ways you can maximise your passion for social change while creating opportunities for your business to differentiate itself. Maybe your business is the anti-*Amazon* and has the least amount of packaging around its products and never uses plastic. Maybe your products cost more because you will only use delivery drivers that use electric cars.

Whatever your cause is, you can use it as an opportunity to get your message out there alongside your business. But a word of caution - make sure if you are talking the talk, you are walking the walk. If you are posting about the importance of BLM yet have only white men working for you or in your senior team, then you need to look at whether you are part of the solution or part of the problem.

39. Photos

A picture can tell a thousand words, right?

Do not underestimate the importance of visuals. Print and online publications have a picture desk that will pay big bucks for a single photo. You don't need to make big bucks. You just need to get a photo that will encapsulate your message and feature your brand.

You want your photo to tell a story. These photos create engagement and get people talking and are the most valuable. So don't just be thinking about photos of your product.

Zara did a good job with their photos during lockdown when they sent their fashion models clothes to wear at home. They got the models to take the photos of themselves in their homes and gardens meaning they told a very topical story during a difficult time.

To mark the launch of the *Doctor Who* exhibit in Olympia, they staged four Daleks crossing Westminster bridge and got photos of them with Big Ben in the background.

If you have a photo of something unusual but topical, think about how you might be able to use it creatively. I would also always be encouraging your customers to tag your business into their photos. You never know when they might get a photo that really captures people's imagination.

TOP TIP - If a newspaper is going to use a photo they will want it in landscape so make sure most of your photos are shot like this. If it's in portrait you are making your life harder. The same applies for video.

40. Video

Video is pretty similar to photos. If you ever have footage of people in your shop/class or business that could get featured on *You've Been Framed*, use it!

The same applies if you have CCTV of people doing something illegal or capturing someone having a baby or a pet doing something cheeky. Perhaps you have security footage of bad weather that is incredible to watch. When people talk about using video in PR they often think about creating funny content or interviewing people, but often they are sitting on more valuable and engaging video without even realising.

TOP TIP - One thing I would say here is that video should be all over your social media channels. It needs to be on your website and on *YouTube*. Producing your own video content will give you an incredible advantage over any of your competitors and will also be the most effective way you can control the narrative of your business and own your own stories. Make sure you have videos explaining all the key parts of your business - the who, what, where, why and when.

Then think about how you can create regular video content using the ideas in this book. How-to guides, top ten lists, product demonstrations, behind the scenes, a day in the life. All of that is the best way to showcase who you are and what you do.

41. Stunts

PR stunts are a planned event designed to attract attention to your brand. It needs to generate news interest in your product or service. It can't just be completely random.

In my experience, PR stunts can be fairly risky. They normally cost more money than you think they will, and if the news agenda of the day is busy and you don't land media coverage it can feel incredibly disheartening.

But when they do work, they have a long history of creating talkability and buzz around something.

It's a running joke in PR that if you want to do a stunt you can float something down the River Thames. The reason this stunt has been repeated in every possible variation over the last 50 years is because you can do something humorous and attention-grabbing by travelling down the river with it and you can also guarantee a good photo opportunity.

Madame Tussauds did a great stunt when they moved Harry and Meghan from the royal family section of their exhibition. They created photos and videos and raised awareness of their museum really easily. They also did a similar trick by making Boris Johnson wear a *Baby Bjorn* when his son was born.

In 2018 *NowTV* wanted to highlight the 25th anniversary of *Jurassic Park* so erected a giant statue of

Jeff Goldblum posing sexily in front of Tower Bridge. It was nearly 10 ft tall and 23 ft long and weighed 331lbs. Google it. It certainly caught people's attention and also guaranteed photo and video content.

Cadbury's Crème Egg café was a pop-up event that ran in Soho in 2016 and was a great way to encourage people to think about *Crème Eggs* while also having fun and creating content.

The key to a good stunt these days is to do something that will mean people create content for you. Everyone in the *Creme Egg* café took photos and shared them and helped to create a buzz that lasted well beyond a day of media coverage.

My advice is to work with a professional and do it properly. But that's not to say it needs to cost the earth. I did a fairly cheap stunt once for some divorce lawyers where we parked a billboard outside the *Strictly Come Dancing* studios. We wanted to play off the fact that the series had the 'Strictly curse' and that its couples kept divorcing. So the billboard said: 'Partner waltzed off?' and promoted their divorce services. That only cost us for the billboard, which wasn't too pricey, and only needed to be up long enough to get media attention.

42. Merchandise

Everyone loves a freebie, and if you can make merch that people will use in a way that will draw attention to your brand while communicating your key messages, you are onto a winner.

Water Babies give away sun shades for cars with their branding on. This is perfect as it's something that can be useful for all new parents. They get people to do their car advertising for them by providing free merchandise that someone will actually use.

Colchester Zoo do this with car window stickers really well and there isn't an office in the country that doesn't have giant *Sports Direct* mugs. *Baby Ballet* classes let you buy your own *Baby Ballet* Twinkle bear. My eldest still loves his Twinkle bear. News organisations often have their branding on the umbrellas that reporters use – the perfect way to get the *Sky News* logo on the *BBC* when both reporters are at the same location reporting on the same story.

If you are an *Instagram* coach, give away selfie sticks with your branding on them. If you are a PT, get t-shirts or workout vests with your branding all over them. If you are a nutritionist who is passionate about clients drinking water, then give them branded water bottles. If you are a VA, maybe you could send branded planners to clients. Think about whether you could get your brand in front of your ideal client through merchandise that they will use again and again. Try and think creatively.

43. Comment on local events

This is when you take something topical that is happening in your local area or the area that your customers are based in and offer to comment on it.

Maybe it's a new housing development, or the news that a *John Lewis* store is coming to town. Maybe a local person has been involved in a scandal or a crime, or there has been a rise in dog theft or the local pub has closed after 100 years. If it is something that impacts your customers and you can offer some insight into how it will impact the community, you should offer yourself to journalists as someone who can provide a comment.

44. Innovation

I have worked with many people who seem to think they do something innovative and unique. Few do. But when they are genuinely providing solutions and pushing boundaries no one else has, it's interesting to customers and industry press. It may even be interesting to nationals if it is genuinely a really innovative way of solving a problem.
Think about how *Amazon* have tested delivering parcels via drones.

Are you using technology and automation in a way that no one else has even considered yet? Can you do something at the touch of a button? If you do, that could be a story.

45. Exceptional customer service

Stories of exceptional customer service can not only make the news, they can go viral really quickly. An American flying with *Jet Blue* airlines posted on social media about how disappointed he was that he had to check in at the terminal without a *Starbucks*. So the quick thinking social media team organised for him to have a *Starbucks* from the other terminal waiting for him on the plane.

Sainsbury's responded to a letter from a three-year-old complaining about the fact that their tiger bread looked more like a giraffe pattern than a tiger. So *Sainsbury's* changed the name on the label and responded telling her - and the press - that it was her letter that had prompted the change.

Think about the creative ways you have or can go above and beyond for your customer in responding to their needs. If they leave something at your restaurant how can you track them down to return it as quickly and easily as possible? If you have any interactions with children and they leave a toy or comforter, then help them get it back as soon as possible. If you run a party planning business or a children's class and it's fancy dress week, keep some spares around for the parents and kids who forget.

I once got on the wrong bus in Norway. I was supposed to be getting one to the airport, but the driver was quite dismissive of me when I got on, so even though I wasn't entirely sure I was on the right

bus I figured it must be ok, because he had waved me on. I was blonde at the time and people had thought I was Norwegian the whole time I was there, so he hadn't realised I wasn't a native (I do not look Scandinavian at all but I was quite flattered by this assumption until this point).
When we arrived back at the bus depot and I was the only one still on the bus, he asked me again where I was going, and his face went white when I said the airport. I promptly burst into tears - I was 19 at the time and did not speak Norwegian at all. He meanwhile looked tearful too!

He was so apologetic and seemed completely mortified. He spoke to the bus manager and we all stood in a car park in the middle of a forest covered in a foot of snow and they came up with a plan. It was apparent at this point that there was no way I was going to make my flight. But it turned out that the driver's wife worked at a different airport and they had a flight in four hours to London. The bus company booked me onto the flight and the driver then took me in his own car to that airport. It was more than an hour's drive and I was almost certain I would be murdered at many points but I wasn't.

The bus driver had a son travelling in London at the time, and he said that he hoped if the same thing happened to him someone would help him. This happened way before *Twitter* or even *Facebook* but that story would have gone viral if it happened now!

46. How to tips

There is nothing people like better than tips, tricks or hacks. If you work with parents or children, create a short article on your Top 5 Tips to Get Back-to-School Ready. Or The 5 Mum Hacks to make Back-to-School Easier. Or the Things your Child Should Know Before Starting School.

If you work with interiors or fashion, write the Top 10 Must-Have Items to Make Your Home Cosy this Autumn/ Five Essentials for your Winter Capsule Wardrobe.

If you work in music or in entertainment, you could write the Top 5 Tracks to get your Wedding Party Started.

Write it then offer it to a few news or magazine outlets. Make sure you offer it in good time though.

If they don't want it you have lost nothing as it will be great content for your blog/advertorial/ *IGTV/Facebook* lives.

47. Reputation management

I could write a whole other book on crisis and reputation management. But my overwhelming response to any issue is to put your customers at the heart of your response.

Do not put profits first. Do not put ego first. Do not ignore advice from comms experts. Think about what your customers will want from you and then go even further.

If you have had a data breach. If you sold a faulty product. If you have double-booked a wedding venue. If you are making redundancies. If you have broken the law. If one of your staff has brought your business into disrepute with poor behaviour. If you have failed to deliver an item that was needed.

Just apologise and fix it as soon as possible. Don't hope people will go away. Whether it's *TripAdvisor, Google Reviews* or *Amazon* reviews, people will find a way to share the negatives about your business. And on the apology please do not do the 'sorry, not sorry' apologia that many people try. Everyone knows a real apology from a fake one. So don't say 'sorry if you felt sad by what I did'. Say 'Sorry we did this'.

Customers need to know, like and trust your brand. Don't do anything to undermine their trust. Things go wrong, people understand that. The Chinese word for crisis is also the same word for opportunity. Turn what could be a bad story into an opportunity to show how you can go above and beyond.

48. Day in the life

There are a few magazines out there that still have a 'day in the life' section - but they are few and far between. If your job means you have varied and interesting days then share them! Create video content, a blog and even offer an industry journalist the chance to spend a day with you if you have a particularly exciting day (this would be reserved for something like a big event).

If you run a cake business then show us what your day looks like – batch cooking, designing cakes, taking orders, updating your social media, delivering cakes to venues etc. This can be a great way of attracting franchisees if your business is franchised. It gives people a mix of the personal and the professional, so they get to know you while also showcasing your business values and offerings.

49. Behind the scenes

A behind-the-scenes sneak peek is always guaranteed to get interest. If you have a business you run from home or from an office, you can show people what really goes on behind the scenes. Show them the hard work that goes into creating something or making something happen.

Say you run a princess party business. It would be great to see you changing from costume to costume and doing your hair and makeup for each gig as well as entertaining the kids. **Michelle Utz** at *The Hoop* in Stock does this really well on her *Instagram* as she is always posting photos of her chefs behind the scenes. Every photo is guaranteed to make you mouth water.

It's also a great way of creating content from your media coverage. If you are invited on to *BBC Breakfast*, share pictures or footage of yourself in the cab on the way there, in makeup, meeting presenters backstage, etc. If you land print coverage, show yourself buying the newspaper and flicking through until you find the mention of you. If you land radio, film yourself or your colleagues listening to it.

50. EVP

Your EVP is your employee value proposition. Many small businesses think this is something that is just for bigger businesses, but the reality is that any business can offer their employees something that sets them apart in the market.

Perhaps you take your staff away for a weekend as a thank you every year. Perhaps you send personalised gifts to team members that smash their targets or get 5-star *Google Reviews.* Perhaps you hire children's party entertainers when you do training days for your team so their kids have a great time and they can really focus.

Whatever you offer your employees to show your appreciation, you should be shouting about it or getting them to shout about it. It's an easy way to attract new staff and demonstrates your values as a business.

My friend **Nicky Marks** runs quarterly trips for her whole team if they reach their targets. They have literally travelled the world. Dubai, New York, Barcelona, Ibiza, Croatia, Marbella, Glasgow - they have been everywhere. It means she has no problems attracting and retaining staff, plus it shows her that the *Censuswide* team work hard and play hard.

51. Break a record

This is an oldie but a goodie. Find something that ties into what your business is about. If you are a dessert business, then make the biggest doughnut. Or run a competition for someone to eat the most chocolate sauce in one sitting.

With record-breaking attempts you need to work with *The Guinness Book of World Records* and the most essential part is photos and video.

52. Offer location for filming

TV news outlets are always looking for places to film interviews - indoors and outdoors. If you have the space or you have a venue with lots of people visiting who could be asked to interview, then you could be exactly what your local TV producers have been looking for.

If you run a mum and baby class, and they are all happy to be filmed, then reach out to your local TV station and tell them you can help them source interviewees to stories where they might want mums to comment. Maybe you have a café or office with a nice courtyard space that isn't very busy that you can accommodate a camera crew in.

Watch your local news and see where the journalists are conducting interviews and think about whether you could help.

53. Mention of your brand on social media

This should be really obvious but it often isn't. If someone mentions your brand - whether they have tagged you or not - on social media then share it! Respond and engage with them.

You should have an alert set up for mentions of your brand so you can be as responsive as possible. You never know what it might bring.

I was a judge for the 2020 PR Moment awards and one of the best campaigns was by a PR Agency working with Greggs. The agency - *Taylor Herring* - monitored social media for mentions of *Greggs* and their products, and Stormzy mentioned in a tweet what a big fan he was of *Greggs*. The outcome of this was that *Taylor Herring* delivered him a box of Greggs-branded goodies alongside a *Greggs'* black card'. This was clearly a nod to the infamous *Nando's* black card. It was a clever thing to do and cost very little. Stormzy opened the gift in a video on social media and shared his excitement at getting the first *Greggs* black card. Perfect PR.

You don't need celebrities to make this work. Look at normal people and influencers and make their day if they share some love about your brand. Send them a freebie which they will no doubt unbox on social media giving you even more PR and content.

54. Pain points

This is related to the above but slightly different. If you are a chocolate and sweet business, then look out for people who are hungover or tired with a new baby and courier them over some freebies.

If you have an industry awards night with loads of your idea clients there, then plan to send them croissants and bacon sandwiches for breakfast the next morning at the office. Go out of your way to wow your customers.

55. Babies

People love babies. If you can use your own babies or other people's babies in your PR and content then you should. People love reading about babies and will engage with content that features with babies more than other forms of content.

You may think 'how on earth can I use babies to boost my brand awareness', but there are loads of opportunities. You just need to be creative. For example - do you have any employees that have new babies? How are you supporting them during maternity leave? How are you supporting their return to work? Could you organise a Christmas party for your employees and their families? A Christmas party for kids?

Do mums ever use your products on their babies even though they weren't designed for them? Can you create cute company uniforms for staff members' babies? Logo t-shirts on babies look so cute!

56. Dogs

I could pretty much repeat the above but change the word baby for dog. People might love dogs even more than they love children. Since lockdown there has been a huge increase in dog ownership across the world. Take advantage of this.

If you have been looking for an excuse to get a puppy, or better still a rescue dog, then this is it! Get a company dog. Share its story. Dogs will give you endless amounts of content. They will mean that you connect with a whole new audience. When I worked in local newspapers a dog, cat or cute rabbit picture would always help boost circulation figures.

In 2015 *ASB Bank* did a stunt involving dogs that went fantastically well. They used three dogs to as ball boys in an Auckland Open match between Venus Williams and Svetlana Kuznetsova. The dogs did a fantastic job and the videos and photos were just brilliant.

Brands have been using dogs in their advertising for years - which genius hit on the idea of using adorable puppies to sell toilet roll? Which toilet roll brand do you gravitate towards? How about the genius who realised you could use a dog to market household paint? What's the first paint brand that comes to mind? Think about how you can use your dog in your content. Maybe you have a story about a dog doing something remarkable with your product.

Maybe they have found something or rescued something or been a great support to someone.

57. Cats

If you have ever seen the *Netflix* documentary *Don't F***k With Cats* then you will know how much people love cats. (If you haven't seen it then I highly recommend it. It isn't really about cats but a murder. For those of you that have seen it please call Deanna and John if ever I get murdered.)

If you can use cats in your product photography or social media ads, do it. It will probably sell out.

58. Competitors

We have all seen it online: someone writing passive aggressive social media posts and emails about someone who has wronged them in business - stolen their idea, worked with them and then left, copied something they did or criticised them. While a little bit of controversy can put you on the map in the right circumstances, I would not advise that anyone gets into a spat like this online.

If someone copies you, people realise it. You don't need to tell everyone. The likelihood is that you will be the bigger brand and the optics aren't great when someone is seen to be kicking the little kid - regardless of whether they are right or not.

My advice is to take the high road and keep your brand clean. Shrug your shoulders and remember that imitation is the greatest form of flattery. When *M&S* had a pop at Aldi for copying their Colin the Caterpillar cake, they creates a lot of chat around the cake, yes. But neither business came off well, and *M&S* probably came off worse even though they were in the right. Because some people can't afford the *M&S* version of the cake. So they buy the budget version. They also highlighted that you could buy the cake cheaper elsewhere!

And as for *Aldi* - they looked like they can't come up with any original product ideas. A narrative that's already out there that was reinforced by this. There are plenty of people having birthdays that need cake. I don't think *M&S* needed to be that worried about the market share. They should have thought more about their brand reputation. Everybody knows that Aldi sells cheaper versions of recognisable products that are dressed up in packaging to make them look similar. It's Aldi's brand identity. There was no need for *M&S* to come out fighting like this and it made it look like they were punching down.

59. Q&A with your top team

Who are the employees that you can't live without? Share what they do and why they are so important to your business. Make sure everyone in your business is on your social channels in some way. There shouldn't just be one face. Because even if it is your business, everyone knows that you aren't doing it without support.

You may even find that someone in your top team develops their own niche and profile that you can then use to target even more customers.

This kind of content is perfect for *LinkedIn*. A lot of people ignore *LinkedIn* and focus on the more consumer-focused social media channels like *Facebook* and *Instagram*, but *LinkedIn* is where you want to be if you have an ideal client that is a professional with a bigger budget.

It's also far easier to get attention with informative and engaging content on *LinkedIn* as there is much less competition that there is on a platform like *Instagram*. Think about what your team can bring to the table here.

60. Paper reviews

Radio hosts and TV shows are often after paper reviewers. If you are really involved with the news agenda and passionate about a topic that you know will be in the press, then offer yourself as a paper reviewer.

If you are a stylist, you can offer your insight into the best-dressed after the Oscars. If you are in education, you can offer yourself up to do a paper review around results day. This isn't an opportunity for everyone as you will need to able to think on your feet and potentially debate your ideas live. But paper reviewers who perform well can be invited back time after time and secure regular slots with broadcasters.

If this is something you are interested in, then my advice is to watch and listen to shows that do a paper review for a few months, and then pitch yourself to a producer or even presenter when you know there is a topic in the media that is relevant to your area of expertise. If they think you can add value they will be more likely to book you in for a slot.

61. #journorequest

I LOVE #journorequest. It can be the quickest and easiest way for your to get some media exposure while also learning about how news works and what journalists are after. Journo requests are where journalists put a shout-out on social media for someone to help be a part of their story.

They may need an expert to talk about something. They may need a case study. They may need a location. They may need a product. It could be anything.

How it works is that they tweet under the hashtag #journorequest with what they need and wait for people to respond. There are also *Facebook* groups where you can find lists of #journorequests for you to look through.

In my *Facebook* group **Get Seen, Get Heard** I share journo requests nearly every day that I have found on Twitter or *Facebook* or have been sent by contacts in the industry. My group is just for business owners to talk about PR opps but there are other groups - paid ones - on *Facebook* that allow journalists to share their own requests direct with the group. The best one out there is Lightbulb.

They are a great opportunity to build a relationship with journalists who might be working for a target media outlet for your business. They also give your great TV experience. It can be tricky sometimes to get your business mentioned, but most of the time journalists will be open to it, especially if your business is in some way linked to the story.

What I would say is that you shouldn't JUST rely on #journorequests. It's great to be reactive and get good media exposure for your brand when opportunities come your way, but it's not a substitute for a proactive approach.

62. Annual charity day

Pick a date and make it your annual charity day. You could do anything you want here. Maybe you and your staff go and volunteer at a charity. Maybe you organise an event that raises money for a good cause. Maybe you work with other local businesses to do a fair or community fun run. Be imaginative and every year try to do more or raise more money than last year. Get photos and video from the event or whatever it is that you do.

But whatever you do, never have a giant cheque made. Back in the 00's the novelty cheques were in every photo offered to local newspapers. Remember the story needs to be about the people benefitting from the cash you are raising. Your business is the supporting actor. The beneficiaries should be the focus of any press activity and social media content.

63. Product launch

Are you launching a new product? Then talk about it! Ask for ideas before your launch it. Test it with some of your good customers. Get feedback from staff. Tease your audience with information about it. Explain why you have launched it - was there demand? Is it to make your customer lives easier? Then ask people what they think of it and how it could be even better.

A good way to create buzz around a launch is to limit supply. If people are struggling to get hold of something it can mean that they start wanting it even more. So start an internet frenzy! Anything to get people talking about your new product.

Pop stars often have their new music leaked online. This can then become news as they react to the leak while also reminding people that something new is coming. It can even give people a taste of what is to come.

64. Budget day

Budget day is always BIG news. There are winners and losers. VAT can increase and decrease. Products can be subjected to more or less tax or even subsidies.

Think about how the outcomes of budget day may impact your customers and how they will be feeling. Think about how it will impact your business and other businesses like yours, whether that's small businesses or those in your industry.

Think how it will impact families like yours. Especially if your ideal client is like you. **Lauren Elliott**, the owner of *Music Monsters*, ended up being featured in a double page spread in a national newspaper after budget day, talking about her business and the impact the announcements will have on it.

It's big news, so if you can make it work then do try. Don't forget your local radio stations who might be interested in the impact on their listeners too.

65. Valentine's Day

Journalists are inundated with press releases around Valentine's day and they are virtually all ignore, so I would focus on creating some fantastic content or an event rather than trying to secure media coverage.

People wait longer before getting married now, and are more likely to get divorced, so the singles market is a large one. If you think your ideal client occupies this space then think about how you can make their day a little easier. Do something that makes your employees feel positive and to show that your business has a human face.

Don't just wish everyone a happy Valentine's Day, think about how you can really connect with your audiences. Don't make it about your products but about an experience.

Another route is to consider what kind of content you could provide that could make people laugh. Humorous con-tent about the realities of trying to have a romantic evening with young children could do well and would also give you the chance to let your audience see behind the brand.

66. Set up an event

Events are a lot of hard work to put on, but there is nothing better than getting a lot of likeminded people in a room talking about something they are passionate about.

If you are in the fitness industry, you could create an event for others that work in your industry but aren't your competitors. You could have a PT, a yoga expert, a running coach, a dance instructor, a physio and a nutritionist all scheduled to speak at the same event. Then you could invite people to come and listen.

You could set up an expo and get lots of different people to have stands showing their goods, while also having a range of speakers on different stages.

Events can be as big and as professional as you want them to be. But they don't have to be. They could even be a mostly networking event on a smaller scale or you could take them online.

Your event could be paid or free and you could include time to network as part of it.

You could organise something around a specific topic or invite people to provide training to your audience.

You could do anything you want. The key is to set out what you want to achieve from the event and what your budget is at the start and to stick to it. And remember that getting people to buy tickets is the hardest part. So remember to include this in your budget and plan!

67. Speak at an event

If you don't have the energy, enthusiasm or skills to organise an event then just offer to be a speaker at someone else's event. Look into events where your ideal client will be and contact the organisers with a topic in mind and a short bio.

If you have an established audience that might be interested in coming to the event, then let the organisers know as they may want to leverage your audience to increase attendance.

If you don't feel ready to do a whole speech at an event, then offer yourself up as a panellist. This is a great way to get involved without being the centre of attention.

Some people find speaking in front of an audience easier than others, but the number one way to get good at public speaking is to practise. If you haven't had much experience speaking to an audience, then look at ways you can get this experience. Doing social media lives is a great confidence booster and it can help you to really work on what your message is. I have a freebie that helps with speaking skills on my website – www.enlightenpr.co.uk – download it if you think it can help.

68. Blog for someone else's website

If you are good at blogging and you enjoy it, then a good way to raise your profile and share your expertise is to offer to do a guest post on someone else's blog.

This is a great way of tapping into someone else's audience and they may well return the favour. If you can do a quid pro quo with you doing one for someone, and them doing one for you in return, that's going to be a way of connecting both of your audiences and building links on your website.

My advice is to find someone that works in your industry but isn't a competitor, and to make sure that your topic is one where you can really add some value to the audience. You also need to be ready to help promote the content on your social media channels and create video and images to drive people to consume it.

69. Create a podcast

Everyone seems to have a podcast these days, and for good reason. It's a great way to keep in touch with your audience. Podcasting is the perfect trojan horse for your brand, as people can download the podcast to learn about one thing, but actually be learning about you, your business and your products at the same time.

I launched a podcast in 2019 called *The Case Files* for a legal brand. We managed to get more than 100,000 downloads and reached the top of the iTunes chart. We did this by doing something no one else in the legal industry was doing - we did a legal podcast that wasn't about the law. It was instead about our clients. We told real-life stories of people who had been forced to use a lawyer after something tragic had happened in their lives.

We allowed the clients to talk about their experiences themselves and used the lawyers to chip in towards the end of the podcast to share insights into how they worked with the client to get a good outcome. We covered incredibly powerful stories, from victims of child abuse, clinical negligence, discrimination, road traffic accidents and more.

There are two things that you need to be able to do to have a successful podcast. First, you need to be able to define your audience and create content for them. Do not create content to share what you want to share with people. It's not the right platform for that.

Instead think about what they will be interested enough to download and go from there.

Second, make sure you don't run out of steam. Plan for 20 episodes, and if you think you can fill 20 episodes then you are probably in good shape. If you can't think of 20 different guests or topics that you feel excited to share with people, don't make a podcast. Instead look at idea number 70.

There are plenty of people out there who can teach you how to set your podcast up from a tech perspective, but not many that will help you market it. That's because this is the hardest part and people are still learning. But if you have an audience already, that's the first part of the job done.

My advice is to create a lot of assets to use to promote each episode. Trailers, videos, reels, images etc. Maybe even blogs. Treat each podcast episode as a media appearance and do some behind-the-scenes content too.

70. Guest on podcasts

If setting up and creating a podcast seems like too much hard work at the moment, why not guest on other people's instead?

This is the perfect way to get your message out there without having to build a podcast brand. Listen to the types of podcast your ideal clients will download and look for ones that have guests.

If you are struggling to find ones to target, then ask your current audience what their favourite podcasts are.

Then reach out to the presenters and offer to be a guest. Tell them you will help promote the episode and suggest a topic you could talk about and maybe even offer to provide their listeners with a discount to sweeten the deal.

71. Big numbers

Fun facts about your business can create rich and very visual content. You can use them to illustrate your values and to remind people about the scale of your business.

An example of this for a leggings designer might be working out how much fabric you have used on the last 12 months. It might be the length of 100 football pitches. This simple fact sends the message that your leggings are really popular.

Or working out how many hours you have spent working on something to make sure that it's perfect. That shows that quality is incredibly important to your business.

You can also use numbers to demonstrate your growth by telling stories about how you did 10 orders in your first year and now you do 2,000 a year. You can also show growth by talking about how many people you have supporting your business. If you run events, then show people how many miles or steps you walk on events days. That sends the message that you have been on your feet working to make sure things run smoothly all day.

Numbers give you a proof point so your audience can understand what you mean when you say that quality is a priority for your business. They give evidence to your growth.

If you want people to work with you or buy something from you, then talk about how many people have already done it before. When people say you should keep on top of your numbers in business, that's normally meant as in keep across your financials - which is certainly essential if you want to run a profitable business. But the more interesting information coming out of your business will be the other numbers.

72. Any outliers in your field

Do you have any outliers in your business? By that I mean do you have someone that doesn't fit the 'mould'? Are you the only male baby massage teacher in the UK? Are you the only female working in a construction company? Are you the youngest person to have passed a qualification in your industry? Are you the only grandmother running a phonics franchise? If you or someone in your team is an outlier in their field, then use this as an opportunity to profile them.

If they are incredibly rare then I would offer a profile piece to a national journalist about why they decided to work in a profession that wasn't the norm for someone like them. Maybe you are a former model who has retrained and now run your own plumbing business after you saw a gap in the market? Maybe you run a domestic cleaning business and you have one man working for you and a thousand women.

Outliers will draw attention to your business while also giving you the opportunity to highlight how great your job is, how rewarding it is to help your customers and how you like to have a diverse and inclusive workforce. Think about how you can tell the story to maximum effect across multiple channels.

73. D&I initiatives

I'm really passionate about diversity and inclusion, and while it's something most big businesses heavily invest in, smaller businesses are now playing catch-up.

The evidence shows that diversity in your business will benefit your bottom line. It also helps you avoid repute-tional disasters because you have enough people in the room to tell you if you are missing the point.

I used to volunteer as a magistrate, and while there were a lot of women on the magistracy, there weren't a lot of women under the age of 50. I would say that nearly every magistrate I sat with was hard-working, fair and open to listening to every argument. But the make-up of the magistracy is overwhelmingly older than those who are being prosecuted. It is also a lot whiter and a lot more middle class. That isn't to say that people were prejudiced or were discriminatory. They weren't at all. But there were times when they didn't necessarily see the whole picture because their life experience didn't match that of the people that were in the court room.

However many D&I courses you take and however good your intentions are, you can't truly put yourself in someone else's shoes very easily.

If you want to attract a diverse range of customers to your business, then you need to start with a diverse range of staff and suppliers. That's different ages, sexes, ethnicities and backgrounds.

After you decide to commit to creating a diverse workforce – and therefore customer base - you can then look at how you will do it. You might decide to recruit in a way that you haven't done before. You may decide to set yourself targets. If you have a male-dominated business and you want to attract more women, think about what your employee value proposition could look like to help you do this. Do you offer flexibility? What's your culture like? Do you offer enhanced maternity pay? Think about how your business presents itself - do you just use stock images of a certain type of person? If you are only using images of white men on your website, you will probably find that only white men will apply for jobs at your business.

Once you commit to creating a diverse and inclusive business, then share what you are doing with your audience. Think about the barriers to entry for people and how you might be able to provide extra support to anyone from a different background. Use your audience and ask them for ideas as well. If you are genuinely committed to diversity then you can comfortably start the conversation and see where it leads you.

74. Be a bit silly

One of the best examples of a PR and advertising campaign is *Diamond Shreddies*. In 2008 the internet was almost broken with people talking about *Diamond Shreddies.* They story is that in a focus group for *Shreddies* someone quipped that they weren't square-shaped, they were diamond-shaped. *Shreddies* then rebranded as Diamond Shreddies without changing their product one bit. A silly joke turned in to a huge PR story across the world. The product was the same but the branding changed. There was even a 'combo pack' that contained the square shaped and diamond shaped versions. The tone of the campaign was silly and ironic yet approachable. It revitalized sales with an increase of 18%. A simple change in perspective can work wonders.

Innocent Smoothies did something similar in 2019 when they capitalised on the notorious 'what colour is the dress' internet phenomenon. They created a new juice called 'Bolt from the Blue' which was actually green. This created a social media storm with consumers insisting it was green while Innocent stood firm saying it was blue. *Dulux* paint even got involved by saying it looked like their shade 'crushed pine 3 which was a green shade'. Then Duncan from pop band Blue got involved insisting it was blue.

Being a bit silly can get some real talk value for your brand. Have a think about whether you have anything in your business you can 'rebrand' or give a new name. Be careful with this one – it needs to be suitable for your business, and you want to create an effect of knowing irony rather than actually looking stupid…

75. Sustainability

If you have some sustainability initiatives within your business, talk about them with your audience. Sustainability is a no longer a unique selling point for businesses, but it is something that demonstrates your values.

If you are committed to reducing packaging on your products then explain that to your customers. Make a short video explaining how and why you package your products the way you do and ask for feedback and suggestions.

If you are committed to reducing the carbon footprint of your business, or you have gone paperless, then tell that story to your audience. Explain what prompted you to take the decision and how that has changed things for the better.

Earlier on in the book I talked about the value of fun facts and big numbers. If you can work out how much paper you will save by going paperless for a year, share that with people.

Share videos and content around how to take care of your products and remind people if they can wash at 30 rather than at 60 and the difference that can make.

If your products are priced slightly higher than others on the market because of your commitment to sustainability, share that story. It demonstrates your business values far more than just writing them on your website.

76. Give more than they ask for

One sure-fire way to get people feeling warm and fuzzy about your brand is to give them more than what they bought. Lots of brands do this with discount codes, but the most successful way of doing it is to offer a genuine freebie - a mini pack of sweets goes down well with me. Picture it in your head - what would make you feel more warmly towards a brand: a 10% discount code, or an unexpected free gift of chocolate with your order? What if that free chocolate cost LESS than 10% of an average order?

If you can afford to, you could think about sending a free gift like this - or send a copy of your book or a free product. Give people a month's free membership to your group. Think about the ways in which you can give people what they might need as well as what they want. Any merchandise you have could be good here. Pencils, keyrings, magnets etc.

You can guarantee a lot of people will love a freebie so much they share it on social media, and even if they don't, you will have won a customer's heart for life.

77. Family business

If your business is a family business, then there is always the opportunity to use that as an angle for PR. If you are a husband and wife team then you can share stories about what that's like, make it part of your branding and even offer advice to other people who are considering working with their other half. If you are a mother-and-son team then share that! Talk about why you work together, what drives you nuts and what you love.

Family business stories can always make nice features for nationals – especially if you can have a bit of banter and take it on the chin if your partner or child moans about you or shares funny stories.

78. Seasonal events

If there is a seasonal that ties in with your business, then it's an opportunity for your brand. If you can offer advice and how-to guides that will help people navigate a seasonal event, then do it! Also think about the pain points for your customers prior to them becoming your ideal client.

Pampers and baby brands target pregnant women. They aren't going to buy their products immediately, but they will fit the profile soon!

If your target audience is university students think about how you can reach them through exam results time. Can you offer mindfulness sessions? Webinars or videos explaining clearing?

Ruff and Tumble make dog drying coats. If your dog gets wet in the rain, you wrap them up like a mummy in a drying coat, and ten minutes later they have warmed up and dried off. But every year, they show people how you can also use the coats to keep your dog cool in a heatwave. In this instance, the brand took a seasonal event that everyone always talks about - the hot weather. Then they thought about what their ideal clients are talking about - how to keep their dogs cool. Then they created loads of content and how-to videos explaining how they can help you do it.

A baby class near me called *MyGym* has a ten minute period at the end where the parents are encouraged to leave the children with toys on the other side of the room. It's called 'separation time' and is often the only time that mums with young babies get an opportunity to safely leave them. It's as great way of the kids building confidence and the parents learning how their child responds to them not hovering by their side like a helicopter. *MyGym* staff could easily use their expertise in helping children and parents to learn about separation to create a range of content online and even pitch for editorials.

If you are a shop that supplies prom dresses, shoes, or suits, then create content around finding the perfect dress/shoes/suit. If you sell lunchboxes or school bags for young children, create content that helps mums get their kids ready for school – checklists of what you need to know and buy, or a guide to getting your child to tell you about their day.

Take advantage of the what's topical at different times of the year for your ideal client.

79. Death of the...

Media outlets love a story about how people don't do something anymore, or about how old people or young people don't do something anymore. Do any of these headlines ring a bell?

Death of the English Breakfast,

Death of the Family Dinner,

Death of the Housewife.

My former colleague **Harriet Scott** runs an agency called *Ginger Communications.* They recently did a story for a client about how young people don't use emojis. It made every newspaper and was talked about for days on multiple media outlets. So if you have a product or service that has had its day, or you have noticed that people shop differently or have different needs, then think about how you could create a 'death of the' story.

80. Return of the…

The media also love a good comeback. Has something come back into fashion? Are kippers for breakfast making a comeback? Are all the cool kids into crocheting? At the moment, with the 90s very much (back)in fashion, the media have enjoyed talking about the return of 90s culture. From scrunchies to butterfly tops to baggy clothes.

Are you being asked to stock something or create something that hasn't been asked for in decades? If so think about doing a 'return of' story.

81. Top 10

Everyone loves a top ten list: Top 10 *Britney Spears* songs. Top 10 *Seinfeld* episodes. Top 10 gifts ideas for under 5s. Especially if you have data to back it up (see earlier idea 15-17). They create debate and comments sections are likely to go insane afterwards with people disagreeing with you (some content sites seem to deliberately present controversial views or rankings to get more clicks and more engagement, which does actually work - but don't do this. It just looks cheap!).

But if you really want to get your PR messaging across you need to go deeper than just the best or most popular things. You need to talk about why they are the best or most popular.

'Top 10 reasons couples argue' is a good one, as it gives you a way to explore how often they argue, who starts it, who says sorry quickest, how long the argument lasts, etc. 'Top 10 things you didn't know before you were a parent' is another good one that gives you the opportunity to talk about the changes parenthood brings.

It doesn't have to be the best either. It could be the worst. These listicles can be interesting to journalists and also be interesting to your audience. Just don't make them clickbaity. Make sure you give actual advice.

82. North/south divide

The newspapers love a good opportunity to reinforce stereotypes with north vs. south divide stories, from how hot they like their curry to how much their houses cost. You can do some desktop research to create a story or you can look at your customer data.

My advice is to only do it if it adds value to the customer and tells an authentic story.

83. Gender divide

Do this if it highlights something you want to help change. But if it's that women think about sex less than men, don't.

I hate playing into gender stereotypes. It can get you media coverage, but ask yourself whether that's the kind of media coverage that's right for your brand.

84. Brand ambassadors and advocates

Brand ambassadors tend to be people that you help and encourage to speak highly of your business. I have always taken the view that you want everyone that your employ and work with to be an ambassador for your business. They should be a living embodiment of your culture and values, recommending you and sharing your successes on social media without you needing to ask. If you have 200 employees most of your social media posts should be liked or shared 200 times if you have a highly engaged workforce.

Brand advocates are similar but are normally customers who are passionate about your business. They are highly satisfied customers who actively go out of their way to promote your business because they love it. I am a brand advocate for so many businesses. If I like something I share and support it, especially if it's a small business. Customers will often like and follow your brand on social media as they are looking to build a deeper connection with a brand they already support.

You want to make it as easy as possible for brand ambassadors and advocates to communicate about your business. You don't want them selling, you want them sharing and they can do it via their social media channels, emails, one to one communications or via their websites. You want them to share your stories, share your news and to talk about your brand.

So you need to give them the tools and prompts to do this. Make sure your social media content is shareable. Create a community online for people who are supporters of your brand. Jenny Guertin from Sharkie and Bear is the most fantastic example of this. Get in her *Facebook* group and watch how she does it. She sells earrings and has created a whole army of brand advocates.

One of the easiest ways to do engage your staff is a simple newsletter or Town Hall event sharing information with your staff and making sure they are the first to know.

85. Snowball

This is something so many people don't do but really should. If you end up in the national media, tell your local media - if you tell them soon enough they will likely want to cover the story as well.

Very often a story can start to snowball and as soon as one media outlet covers it, they all want to follow. So make sure your contact details on your website and social media channels are up to date, and that someone monitors your incoming calls and emails on the day you get any coverage.

86. Build a relationship with competitors

There is nothing more powerful than when multiple organisations put their differences side and work together to highlight an issue. If it's important to your audience, it's probably important to your competitors too.

Think about how you can build relationships with other players in your industry, so if that if ever the need arises you can work together to get your message out there. It also means you can share costs and resources. It's not unheard of for governments to legislate companies out of business. If there are proposals that will impact your business, you want to have allies and a supportive culture so you can respond suitably.

Imagine if the government suddenly said that owners of *Faceboo*k groups needed to get a license to operate at a cost of £3,000. You would want to be able to work with other *Facebook* group admins to respond to proposals.

Also, sometimes there will be media opportunities you can't do. A journalist will love you if you can recommend another expert who does what you do. They might even return the favour one day.

87. Letters to the editor

This is always a great way to get your insight into a topical news story featured even if you didn't manage to be part of the story when it breaks.

Letters pages are still a big thing in newspapers so think of it as a way to share your expertise with your ideal customers. Just make sure you talk about why the issue is relevant to your business.

88. Opinion piece

Lots of publications are interested in opinion pieces - especially if you are able to articulate an unpopular view or give a new perspective on something. If the opinion is one that resonates with your ideal client, this could be a great opportunity for PR for your business.

If you have an area of expertise or life experience that means you have a different opinion on something, then put pen to paper and share it. When you write an opinion piece, aim for around 300 words. Structure it with a strong introduction setting out your point of view, and then use the main body of the article to make three clear points before finishing with a call to action.

Make sure you write it when the subject is topical and feels relevant. Don't hold back, either - be passionate and use your own life experience. Explain why you care and have such a strong opinion on the subject. If you want to talk about parenting, then explain you are a mum or a childcare expert.

If you don't feel confident sharing it to your target journalists, then share it on your blog, in a newsletter or in a social media post. You could even do it as a video. Just make sure that when you are putting across your point of view that you aren't unkind or offensive to anyone else. Be passionate, but don't get aggressive or sarcastic. Keep to your values and focus on educating and informing your audience.

89. Free clinic, advice, webinar

One sure-fire way of getting people interested is to offer them something for free. If you run a restaurant, offer a free tutorial where you break down how to make one of your best dishes. Get people to sign up in advance and collect their email addresses for your database, or just do the tutorial live in your social media channels. It's a way for you to demonstrate your expertise as a chef while also showing your amazing, delicious food. You could reach a new audience by offering them something for free, while also reminding the audience you already have that they need to visit sometime soon. It also gives them a chance to see how much work and knowledge goes into creating your signature dishes.

If you are a service provider, you could offer a free webinar where you teach people how to do something. **Sarah Sangster (@sarah_sangster_sanx)** is a digital marketing pro and she taught a free webinar on how to create stickers for social media stories. It was amazing and in 45 minutes I learnt a genuine skill that I now use to the point of annoying my audience. I told everyone about it and I will always recommend Sarah to anyone with digital marketing needs.

Think about what you can offer people for free that can help them. It's a great way to get known for something and to help people know, like and trust you.

90. Newsletters

Forget your social media reach - your mailing list is much more valuable as you actually own the details. *Facebook* or *Instagram* could shut down your social media channel in a moment and your audience would disappear.

So nurture and love your email list with a regular newsletter. Let them get to know your brand. Don't just sell to them. Make the newsletter worth something to them. Share advice, tops and tricks to help them solve their pain points instead.

Use it as an opportunity to drop in your business values and your purpose. Make sure your business culture comes through.

91. Infographic

I do not think very visually but a lot of people do, which is why infographics can work so well for businesses. If you have some data or some information you want to share, think about creating an infographic. This is a way of telling the story through pictures when you may not have photos. It also makes complex information easier to understand. They can be entertaining and humorous and hold the attention of your audience longer than a normal piece of written content. The more useful they are, the more shareable they are as well.

This can work really well with top ten lists, with how-to guides, when presenting data and facts, and when explaining anything that amounts to a system or process.

If you have ever bought a property, you will know how difficult it can be to understand what's happening, what should have happened, and where you are in the process. If an estate agent or solicitor created a handy infographic to talk you through the steps required to get to your dream house, it would make it easier for you to understand.

Canva is the best place to go to create infographics, and they have a variety of templates available for people that can bring your information to life. Think about creating a few for your website and content, and make sure they are in your brand colours with a small logo, and that they are easily shareable.

92. Influencer

Influencers can be a great tool for PR but the relationship needs to be authentic and you need to share common values. I am always very cautious about using influencers for long term relationships, as you essentially cannot control a person outside of your company the way you can a brand. Celebrities get involved in scandals and demonstrate values that do not align with yours or those of your customers - so you need to do your due diligence in getting to know anyone you might be using and not just be wowed by their follower count. You also need to ensure they have a genuinely engaged audience. Quality over quantity.

PR is essentially storytelling, and influencers can be a great way of amplifying your stories. But make sure you have clear expectations from both sides. **Abi Hugo (@thewhitethistle)** has a podcast and *Facebook* group all about being and working with influencers so if you want to go down this route then I would start with her and do some research.

93. Customer testimonials

These should be a foundation of your content strategy. People want to hear how happy and helpful your product or service was to other people. They want to know how it helped and they want to see evidence for that.

This is even more important if you are buying something more expensive. If I am considering buying some-thing for £5 on *Amazon*, I will probably just go for it. If it's more than £50 I will start looking at reviews and reading how other people found the product.

So every time you have a happy customer ask them for a customer testimonials. A video testimonial is even better. Bigger companies will often come to you with one written for your to amend and approve in the B2B space, which is even more helpful so if you think that might help your customers then consider offering that.

Make sure that testimonials are on your website, sales pages and in your social media content.

TOP TIP - Often it's when you are asking for testimonials that you find out interesting stories about your customers which could make standalone content, or even something for the media.

94. A book or eBook

Writing a book or eBook is the perfect way to PR your business. This is because it's the perfect way to help your audience with a problem or pain point. You may feel like you are constantly sharing information with your audience, but people need to hear the same thing over and over before they really understand what you are telling them. That's why a book can be the best vehicle for your messaging.

If writing a whole book sounds intimidating, then consider an eBook. They don't have to be very long. They could be as little as 5,000 words. If you are a regular blogger, you may find that you can build on some of your blogs quite easily and provide some real value with a book. As long as it helps people, and your book is focussed on the reader instead of you, then you will find an audience for it.

A book is a great way to establish you as an expert in your field and give an added boost to your credibility. It demonstrates that you are a thought leader in your field and gives you an opportunity to talk about your experience and credentials. If you have written a whole book on a subject, you must know what you're talking about.

It can set you out from your competition and allow your audience to really get to know you, what you stand for and what you can do to help people. It's a way to build a connection with people and the nature of a book means that you get the opportunity to talk to people in their own homes!

Books are also evergreen and passive, so once published they can drive constant traffic to your website as well as build your email list and social media followers. You can self-publish pretty easily. I'll happily share how I published this in my blog - but feel free to email me for advice.

There are arguments both sides about whether you should self-publish or get an agent and publisher. I'm not an expert but it appears to pretty much come down to how big your audience is.

95. Speak at local schools

Schools are always looking for guests to come in and speak to their students. It could be to run a workshop or to educate them in an area of the curriculum or to provide careers insights. It's always useful building links in your local community, and your local schools are a great way to do that. If you have an interesting story to tell or a skill you can share with children - whether they are nursery age or about to head to university - reach out to your local schools and offer your services.

Women who can talk about their experience working in STEM (science, technology, engineering and maths) areas are normally quite sought after in schools, as this is an area that statistically far fewer women are likely to go into. It's also an opportunity to highlight alternative career paths like apprenticeships and careers that are somewhat less conventional.

If you have written a book, travelled to help a community in need, climbed a mountain or achieved something against the odds, there are always opportunities to speak at schools. It provides a fantastic way of getting your name out there in the community and making people think of you should they need someone with your expertise.

96. Stop selling a well-selling product

This sounds mad, right? But big brands do this all the time. They decide to stop selling something - then there is public outcry until they decide to bring it back. You even get TV shows and film companies doing this. You control your business, so if you decide to stop selling something or offering a service, you can announce it and then wait to see if there is a response. If your customers contact you and beg you to start selling it again, then you can build up a waiting list and ask your audience if they want you to bring it back. Let the momentum build and then give in to their demands and start selling it again.

You may even find that there is a rush on as people worry that you are going to stop stocking a product they absolutely love. *Pizza Hut* do this to me all the time with their *Cheesy Garlic Tear and Share Bread*. One day they sell it, the next they don't. *McDonalds* are always introducing limited edition menus. Think about what your audience loves and whether you can limit it for a while. If you have a subscription or membership, you could think about limiting your spaces for a while and seeing what kind of momentum and buzz you get from people who want to join more than ever because they suddenly can't.

97. Be a case study

Media outlets are looking for people to use as case studies every single day. Case studies are the lifeblood of news as they help illustrate why stories are relevant to the audience. When the government introduces a new policy or a change to tax rates or benefits, then journalists need real people impacted by these changes to explain what the impact will be. Without case studies, news bulletins can become a series of talking heads. Real people are needed to bring the news to life.

So journalists are constantly looking for people that fit a certain profile and have had a certain experience so they can talk to them and find out more about an issue. This is what a lot of #journorequests are about and can be an excellent way of getting your business mentioned in the media.

I share case study requests in my *Facebook* group most days because if you fit the profile and can add insight to a news story journalists will often happily mention your business, especially if it can be linked to the story in some way. If there was an opportunity for mums to talk about homeschooling during lockdown, then you could offer to be the case study and highlight how hard it has been running your business at the same time. If it's a case study request for women who have suffered postnatal depression, you might want to share your story and talk about how your experience made you want to set up your own business.

Being a case study can be a lot of fun. I have been one quite a few times in my life. Sometimes you will be offered a fee for your time, and my advice is to always ask for a mention or link to your business instead. I have been a case study for the Daily Mail and for The Sun and both times I got my hair and makeup done and the Daily Mail even supplied me with dresses to wear for the photoshoot. It took about half a day and gave me some lovely free photos to use.

You may even have a client or customer that could be a case study. If you are an event planner and you can provide a journalist with a couple who are getting married for a news story, then the journalist will often feature you in the piece as well. In my work for law firms, when we offer one of our clients as a case study, we often do it on the condition that one of our lawyers is featured in the interview too. This puts the client at ease while providing the law firm with some additional brand awareness and all the other benefits that media coverage can bring.

TOP TIP - Don't lie. Don't ever feel pressured to lie or change your story so it fits what the journalist is after. You will get found out and the aim of doing PR is to get people to know, like and trust you. No one trusts a fibber. If you have any concerns that the journalist may not accurately take down what you have said, then ask to read back what you have said after your interview. Most journalists have excellent and accurate shorthand and will write down what you say accurately but often what we say in a chatty conversation with a journalist can look very different when written down on paper. If you have any concerns ask to see what they intend to publish and try and help them to get the story correct.

98. Share a personal story

People like to hear about people. Sometimes something happens and we want to share it. It could be anything. From an issue with your child, to a situation with your elderly grandparents, to a drama with your neighbour. It could be something that frustrates you that you want to raise awareness of, or it could be a truly tragic event that you want to share in the hope that it doesn't happen to anyone else.

There can be a range of reasons behind wanting to share a personal story about your life. You might want to set the record straight, or just want to get something off of your chest. There is no doubt that by sharing the personal side of your life you can build a better relationship with your audience. They will feel they know you better and probably warm to you. You won't just be a name behind a social media account. You will become a real and more rounded person.

You should never share more than you are comfortable with, and your business doesn't have to show your personal life. If you are going through a horrendous divorce and custody battle, you are more than entitled to keep that to yourself. It's your life; you should share what you want. No one deserves to know what's going on behind closed doors. But if you want to share your story, then then it can provide an opportunity to shine a light on an issue and your business.

Sometimes a negative experience can prompt you to take action through your business. You might decide to raise money or volunteer your time or gift products.

If you do decide to share a personal story my advice is to make sure that everyone who is a part of the story is consulted in advance. Some people are incredibly private and might feel uncomfortable. I'd also think carefully around what you want the outcome of sharing your story to be. If it's to fundraise or raise awareness, then make sure you share it in a format that will mean that's possible. So if you share your story online you will need to make sure other people can share it. Sometimes the best way to share a personal story is via a blog. That way you can carefully consider your choice of words and how you tell your story.

99. Competitions

I love a good competition and giveaway! Who doesn't? It's a great way to mark the launch of a new product or to celebrate a milestone in your business. If you can afford to give away a few samples, then this is a fantastic way to get new eyes on your brand.

If you want to place a competition on a website or magazine or newspaper, there are different rules and policies for each media outlet. Some will charge you thousands of pounds to place a competition, while smaller local media may let you run them for free.

Think about who your ideal client is and where they hang out, and then look into the cost implications of running a competition there.

One advantage to running a competition with a highly sought-after prize is that you can use it as a way to encourage people to sign up to your mailing list. The usual GDPR policies will still apply, but it gives you the chance to get emails from people who are already interested in your product so you can retarget them through a *Facebook* ad or email marketing campaign.

If your prize is really incredible then you might even be able to get some media coverage around it before and after. Definitely ask the winners to create content for you to share celebrating their win.

100. April Fools' Day

Every year you will spot a raft or fantastic PR stunts on April Fools' Day. In 2016 *British Military Fitness,* who run nationwide outdoor fitness classes, announced they were running classed for overweight cats. This was accompanied by photos of tubby cats working out. Cue media coverage full of cat puns and lots of attention on the brand which communicates the messaging that they run outdoor fitness classes. I have talked before about how much people love cats - so this was a great idea that was always going to do well.

In 2015 *Tesco* said they were introducing 'bouncy aisles' with trampolines down them so people could jump easier to reach the high shelves.

Using the old everyone-loves-dogs trick, Hunter announced dog wellies, while *Rosetta Stone* announced a course that enables you to learn how to talk to your dog.

Virgin love a good April Fool and in 2015 they announced the glass floor plane. In 2016 it was a fitness coach in their trains. Ant and Dec got in on the act in 2021 by announcing a rebrand saying they wanted to be known as Dec and Ant going forward, while *Interflora* announced mood flowers that change colour depending on how you were feeling.

If you put your thinking cap on early and can come up with a fun idea for April Fools' Day, my advice is to get organised early. Get video and image mock-ups and interviews ready. But most importantly, refine your messaging carefully so you can ensure that the audience gets a sense of your values and what your mission is as well as your sense of humour. Play it as straight as possible and maybe even collaborate with other businesses as well. *Heinz Beans* have collaborated with *Weetabix* and *Innocent* in the past.

PR STRATEGY

BUSINESS OBJECTIVES

PR GOALS	TARGET PUBLICATIONS	APPROACH
3 THINGS HOLDING YOU BACK	3 REASONS WHY YOU ARE THE BEST	DESIRED PERCEPTION

PR STRATEGY

KPI'S

RISKS

BIG DREAM

ASSETS

DEPENDENCIES

WHERE TO START

REVIEW DATES

Thank you for reading! I would love you to share you successes with my *Facebook* group or on my *Instagram* page.

If you have any questions, feedback or suggestions on improving this book or would like to work with me further please email alison@enlightenpr.co.uk

Disclaimer: The information contained within this book is general in its nature and for informative purposes only. It is based on the author's personal experience. The author assumes no responsibility whatsoever, under any circumstances, for any actions taken as a result of the information contained herein.

Acknowledgements

This book couldn't have been done without my husband and editor Matt Carter. He encouraged me and supported me and believed in me without hesitation. I would also like to thank my constant cheerleaders. Nicky Marks, Charlie Day, Lisa Jackson-Hunt, Natalie Tracey, Tom Gardner, Howard Kosky, Caroline Ward, Martyn Beau-champ, Kalle Amanatides and Nicola Atkinson.

Printed in Great Britain
by Amazon

68311570R00095